I AIN'T
TRYING
TO BE
FUNNY

D1558240

*

*

I AIN'T TRYING TO BE FUNNY

DON'T TAKE LIFE TOO SERIOUS, BUT BE SERIOUS ABOUT LIFE

By:- John Wayne Penton, Sr.

*

ISBN 0-9764525-0-2

All photographs were taken by the author and associates. The Book cover and layout were done by the author.

Order or Contact:
www.johnwaynepenton.com

printed in the United State of America

*

Acknowledgement

It has been a long journey in writing this book. The struggle in the journey was mostly within me, convincing myself that I could write. However, I was encouraged by many friends and family members. To them I am grateful.

I want to say thanks to Dr. Paul White for his words of encouragement, He said, "you can write, just write a few line or pages each day and you will finish in no time". I want to thank Bishop T. L. Westbrook for the example he set for me and the encouragement he gave me when I would share with him my dreams.

Thanks to my sister Mildred Grayson who has been a great support and editor. Thanks to Sister Marilyn Delin the Church Secretary, she also helped in editing this book, "I Ain't Trying to Funny".

It would be impossible for me to mention each person by name that played a roll in my life which gave me the experiences to make this book possible. However, I want to give each person I have met on this journey a great heart felt, "Thank You!"

Most importantly, I Thank God for the experiences. I apologize for any mistakes you may discover in this book. Remember I Ain't trying to be funny.

Contents

With a name of John Wayne, I ain't trying to be funny.

Introduction

John sitting on a boat in Hong Kong

TELL YOUR STORY

S itting on a junk, a boat that is called home by thousands in Hong Kong, I told my wife to "get a picture of this." This picture is a sentence in the pages of my life story. A boy raised in Bogalusa, Louisiana, overcoming many odds to write about his personal experiences captured in time to be shared at this time. My story!

Life is a story. Your life is your story. The concern would be, how bold are you to tell your story to others? Most people I have talked with, love talking about the exciting things that have happened in their life, but they are not sure if people want to hear those experiences that impacted their life. Another impeding factor that prohibits people from sharing their life story is that it takes time to tell the intricate details of a story about being, "chased by a thousand blood thirsty cannibals in the darkest parts of the jungle in some exotic place." Certainly, such drama demands an audience. However, with such a story, people usually pay money to sit for several hours to see and hear the adventure. They would visualize the climatic ending as you describe how you thought you were a "goner" when you slipped and fell. I am sure your audience could even hear the thundering sound of thousands of hungry cannibals closing in on you with one thing on their mind...*It's dinner time.* Suddenly, you are lifted to safety by an angel. Yes, this would be a story made for the big screen. If your story is not filled with high drama such as the cannibal experience, yet you are excited about it; then tell it! You may be surprised! Somebody wants to and needs to hear your story.

Life is as a continuum in which negative and positive activities influence you, from the time you are born to the present time. This can be a span of a year to many years. There is a scripture in the Bible, **Romans 8:28:** "And we know that all things work together for good to them that love God, to them who are the called according to *His* purpose." I realize that this scripture is taken out of context and given meaning that was not intended by the Author, but the "His purpose" part suggests God has everything in control, regardless of how it may seem to us in the present. This is why, I am writing this book to bring some perspective to this scripture from my personal experiences in life.

Everybody's got a story to tell. Their life is the story. The question may be who wants to listen to the story. If you think your life is interesting and you have a desire to share, then you must discover your audience, they are waiting to hear your story.

If we look at life as a journey, and journal our experiences as we travel life's highways, which often takes us on detours of uncertain destinations, we will find something worthy to share with people we meet on the same road. It is certain we can learn from those that have been where we are going. When we tell our experiences whether we share them in the form of a book or by word of mouth we are a great source of information and inspiration to those who are searching for answers to the questions of life. This exchange of information may save a life: by telling others, what to avoid or what to expect down the road we have already traveled. Therefore, our experiences may encourage those that are stagnated by fear in the uncertainty of the road ahead. Your story must be real even though it may read like a novel. Your sincerity is what encourages people to use your experiences as an example to motivate them to overcome similar struggles in their life. Your journey is your story.

There is great value in the experiences we have in life, if we could see life more objectively than subjectively. We are subjective when the pain of some mishap that occurred consumes us; or we egocentrically give more attention to the accolades we receive when we do some noticeable achievement. These detractors cause us, sometimes, to miss opportunities to receive or to give. Simply stated, it is being selfish when at a time we are most needy not to ask for help or when we have abundance not to give to ease the needs of others. This attitude is usually because we take ourselves too seriously and we become very selfish and defensive of out current state of being. It has been important to me not to take myself too seriously. It keeps me from stressing over things I cannot control.

When ego is the driving force of our rejection to reasoning, we stand the chance of putting ourselves in danger on life's highway, not caring about the danger in which we find ourselves.

I remember one Sunday I was driving with my family from church; the trip was 30 miles to our home. My wife noticed we were low on gas. She mentioned it to me, but I told her we can make it home without refueling. It really was ego that kept me from taking heed to the voice of reason. I remember very well, the coughing sound the engine made before "giving up the ghost" about six miles from home. As all five of us walked home, I could hear in my mind, my wife saying, "I told you so." She did not have to say it verbally, but it was loud and clear. After getting over the embarrassment of walking through the neighborhood for six miles, it was funny. If I had only listened! It is that way in life, as someone said so well, "hindsight, is always twenty – twenty." The regret is, if I had only listened.

iv

We could be spared some of life's embarrassing moments, if we only listen. The most common rejection of wisdom from our wives is when they try to tell us that we missed our turn and then we continue to drive for another 100 miles before accepting the fact we are lost. Why is that, men? Ego! The point is that ego sometimes causes us not to take the time to hear the wisdom in the stories of our lives, because we take ourselves too seriously. I say, "Don't take life too serious, but be serious about life." We definitely reject opportunity to glean wisdom from others when we think we know everything and we are too serious about preserving our right to be wrong.

Telling your story in a way others can identify with your experiences and discover that you handled the difficulties in life the way they should or could have. Yes, we are different and our experiences are different, but we are human. We laugh, we cry and we find that we have more in common than we have differences.

Writing my story in the form of a book has been challenging. I had to get over many self-imposed fears. One of the greatest fears was that I could not spell very well, and that my grammar had a lot to be desired. I did not want anyone to know I had these limitations. My physical limitation was that it is difficult for me to sit for any length of time and stay focused. Therefore, it was hard for me to sit long enough to write my thoughts.

I invested in gadgets that I thought would help me work through my fears. I thought the tape recorder would work best for me, because I could talk while I was moving and later have my voice transcribed. This idea did not work well for me, because it took more time going back over the tape to hear what I said than to type. Thank God for word processors! I finally realized that I must overcome my fears, and just do it. This book took more time to overcome my fears, than it took to write the words that the book contains. Like one songwriter said, "It's my party and I can cry if I want to." I say it is my story and I can write it if I want to. Now it is your book, I hope you read it because you want to. Enjoy, "I Ain't Trying To Be Funny."

Chapter One

THE BLUE BABY

"Blue baby", my mother told me that was my diagnosis on Wednesday, May 25, 1949, the evening I was born at the Charity Hospital in Bogalusa, Louisiana. The Doctors told her that somehow, I was poisoned during her pregnancy, which caused this sometimes fatal condition. In order to increase the chance of my survival a complete blood transfusion was required. My mother submitted to the Doctors' suggestion, while I lay there newly entered into a world of uncertainty. They took a needle that looked as large as the diameter of my little fragile neck, to make the blood exchange from certain death to a possibility of life with the new blood. I did not know it at that time, but now I know it very well, that God had and has a plan and purpose for me. I was constantly reminded of my miraculous entry into this world, when Mom tried to take me out of the world with her "reckless endangerment" way of correcting me, using nature's botanical flexing rod, known as a "switch." I not only survived the "blue baby" diagnosis, I also

John at 6 years old

1

Standing next to Grandma house

survived the black and blue episodes of Mom telling me, "This is going to hurt me more than it is going to hurt you." If that was true, we should have been crying together.

I am a "baby boomer" and during my adolescent years, the country was struggling with accepting the fact that African Americans were first class citizens and that we demanded our place as equals in a society that had double standards. This was during a time when the civil rights struggle was the order of the day. The blacks were becoming more and more assertive in demanding their equal rights. This was too much for the local Klan in Bogalusa. The cross burning, the drive-by shootings, and employment intimidation were the tactics that were used to keep the blacks in "their place": which was quiet and submissive.

The African American community wanted a piece of the American dream, and they were not going to let things continue as usual. Several people I knew lost their lives in the struggle for civil rights. It was not an option for the blacks to report any crime to the police, because most of the Police Officers were Klansmen. Therefore, we needed a means to protect ourselves.

The "Deacons of Defense" were our in-house police force. These were men that had made up their mind that, "enough is enough." This group became infamous to the whites because they armed themselves with weapons and a determination to protect their community from the rage of the "white man." I felt much safer, knowing that black people were looking out for me. A sense of pride came over me, when I heard about the courageous acts of the "Deacons of Defense."

I knew that one day I would be able to stand proud in the work place, knowing that I was considered to be an asset to my employer instead of a liability. This kept me in the fight for self-determination. Of course the civil rights struggle was a major roadblock that was standing in my way, yet it was not the only obstacle. I had to overcome the stigma of my father being a notorious "good ole Joe" alcoholic.

One of my teachers who was black just told me outright, that I was going to be nothing. She looked at me with disgust and said, "You're going to be just like your Daddy, an alcoholic." This was my motivation, from a negative perspective. I became even more determined to fulfill my dream.

When my Dad got drunk, sometimes he

In front of Walter's Po Boys

3

would bring complete strangers to our house. One night he brought a white man home with him. They had their arms around each other singing some song that drunken people sing, and they seemed to be enjoying what they were singing. They were in another world void of understanding that segregation was a law and not an option. This was a sight to behold for us. We had never seen a white man up close, and certainly we had never seen a white man in our house, except the police. This was better than watching TV, a white man in our house! We thought we were moving up in society to have a white man in our house. We would hide behind the wall that separated the kitchen from the living room, looking fascinated and talking to each other about how blessed we were to be the only black family to have a white man sleeping in our house. He was dressed in a wrinkled suit lying on the couch in the living room. We were brainwashed to believe that the white man had more value than the

On Campus Central High 1966

black man. It was paradoxical to see such a display of unity between two men unaware of the time and place.

The consumption of alcohol was the cause of much of the pain in our family. Now, the consumption of alcohol was the influence that was anesthetizing two men from the pain of racism. I knew this was a dream of a future possibility of two men, black and white enjoying each other without being aware of the color of their skin. I am sure when they both awoke they saw it as a nightmare of regret. I never knew what happened to the man, because when we woke up the next morning, he was gone.

My Dad, Robert T. Penton, Sr.

My Mom, Juanita Jackson

My Dad's Mother Olivia Penton

Mattie and Earnest Smith, Mom's Parents

At the height of the civil rights movement, Bogalusa became a "safe place" for the whites from the north. The northerners would come down to the south and join the civil rights activists. The northern activists were the number one enemy of the KKK, who thought these "northerners" were the ones that were motivating the southern blacks to take a stand against segregation. We were encouraged to see white people openly walk along side the blacks singing, "We shall overcome, some day."

It was during this time, my sister Barbara died of an enlarged heart that was discovered during a physical examination in her senior year of high school. Barbara's funeral was a time to convince the people to continue the fight for justice. Even though, it was not the intention of community to turn her funeral into a rally, it happened. We used every opportunity to get messages to the masses during this turbulent time of social unrest. During the funeral, people were given a chance to talk about the deceased. I remember a white man stood up to speak about my sister. It was surprising, because I knew he did not know Barbara. I knew he was a civil rights activist from the north, but I wondered what he could say about my sister. He began to speak and the words he was saying did not match with Barbara's eulogy. I knew she did not die a hero in the struggle as was suggested by his speech, but she was courageous, because she knew she was dying and that did not stop her from being supportive of the movement in her own way. However, it was inspiring to know that her funeral

7

would be a time to speak words that encouraged all of us to continue the fight against segregation.

I do not recall being down with any major illness as a little boy growing up, other than the blue baby experience. However, I know I have suffered many incidents that could have been life threatening, if God had not protected me. Time after time, I have been ignorant to imminent danger that could have caused death. Just to name a few: I almost picked up a poisonous copperhead snake, thinking it was a pretty colored hose left in the tall grass of a field. Just as I knelt down to pick it up, it slithered toward me and I still do not know how I moved so quickly to avoid being bitten. Another incident that could have changed the course of my life was when an arrow shot from a "homemade" bow hit me in the eye. I lost sight in my left eye for a moment. I ran wildly home unable to see. I certainly could have lost my eye or even died if the arrow had hit a little more to the left. Any of these incidents could easily have made this "blue baby miracle boy" a dead boy.

I ain't trying to be funny, but I discovered electricity. Mom came running into the bedroom after she noticed all the lights go dim and she heard a loud thump like something hitting the wall. It was me being thrown across the room after inserting a metal coat hanger in the wall socket. When my Mom came into the room, she saw my glowing electric personality with my hair slightly raised charged with electricity. I said like Doctor Frankenstein in the horror movie, "It's alive! It's alive!" My curiosity was no less than Benjamin Franklin's when he stood in an open field in the midst of a lightning storm waiting to be hit by lightning. We had something in common: we both had the spirit of exploration. His experiment is written in history books for others to learn. My experiment is written in my book, "I Ain't Trying To Be Funny" for others to learn not to take life too seriously, but be serious about life.

There was a lot of praying going on in our house. I do not believe I would have made it through adolescence without Mom and the saints praying, "Lord save that red boy." I know mom was praying this prayer for me to be saved from going to hell, but I believe God assigned me an angel to make sure I would make it to heaven in one piece. I am sure God told the angels to watch over me. I was just a mischievous kid with a curious mind.

I was not sure who God was, I only knew if you prayed he will hear you. Therefore, I prayed the prayer that mom taught me each night just in case, "Now I lay me down to sleep, I pray the Lord my soul to keep, and if I die before wake, I pray the Lord my soul to take, Amen."

After praying I sometimes wondered if I could tell the exact time I would fall asleep, so I would experiment by trying to hold my arms straight up while lying on my back in the bed so that I could tell the very moment I went to sleep. Well, that is something you will never be able see first hand. Really, I wanted to know, and I ain't trying to be funny.

9

The Projects
Oak Hills Homes Apt. 56

The window to the bed room where the fire started

The front of apartment 56 where I lived at the age of 6 to 17 years

Chapter Two

THE BURNING HOUSE

I once said that "life is not lived by accident nor is death spared by ignorance." This statement I know too well, because I almost lost my life due to a moment of ignorance. When I was seven, our family lived in the projects: Apartment "56" Oak Hill Homes. On a clear warm autumn afternoon I was looking for a lost marble under the dresser in my sister's bedroom. I lit a candle to see into the darkened shadow under the dresser. After searching for a few moments I found the marble. In my excitement, I ran outside and accidentally left the candle under the dresser.

I went back to playing marbles with my friends near the side of the apartments. Then suddenly my friend hit me on the shoulder to get my attention, he said, "Man, y'all must have magic curtains!" At first, I did not know what he was talking about; I thought he was trying to be funny. Then he got more excited, and then I looked in the direction he was pointing. He was pointing at my sister's bedroom window. Sure enough, the curtains were vanishing right before my eyes. I got up quickly and ran toward the back door. My sister, Mildred, was standing in the doorway and was not

11

aware of the fire in the bedroom. Quickly I pushed her out of the way, closed the door, locked it and ran to the bathroom to get water to put out the fire.

I could not find a container to carry water to the bedroom, so I put my mouth to the facet, filling it with water until my cheeks were like balloons. I ran from the bathroom to the bedroom and spit the water into the bedroom inferno. The fire had consumed the dresser and it was just catching on to the bed. I was so afraid. The only thing I could think about was what my Dad and Mom were going to do to me when they got home. The danger of the fire was not as frightening as the pending danger that was yet to come from the wrath of my parents. After all, the fire was destroying the furniture, my sister's clothes, and the toys that Mom had put away for Christmas

Flames engulfed the bedroom, as I ran like the cartoon character "Flash" with supersonic speed from the bathroom to the bedroom with my mouth filled with water. The neighbors saw the fire and quickly turned on the garden hose tying to quench the fire from the outside. I was not going to let them come in because I was afraid they would tell my parents. They knocked on the door and I purposely ignored them. Besides, I was too busy rushing with water in my mouth trying to put out the fire.

Then later I heard a banging on the door and yelling. It was the firefighters, shouting for me to open the door. By this time they successfully had the fire under control, but they needed to get inside to complete their task. I came to the door, and I would not open it because, I was afraid and tired. I put my face to the glass of the back door with tears in my eyes and said, "My mama told me not to let anybody in while she is gone." Of course, they succeeded in getting the door opened. The firemen removed all the badly burned contents of the bedroom outside to the lawn.

My father came home, while I was sitting outside near the smoking mattress. He came near me. I was too tired to run. I knew what was going to happen. He was going to do to me what the fire did not do and that was kill me! I braced myself for the fatal blow. Instead, a gentle hand touched me and then he hugged me. The sweetest words came from my Dad, "Son, are you alright?" This was a defining moment for me with my dad. A man that was controlled all his life by the rage of alcohol, now, he was gentle and understanding. I realized then, that this was the real man behind the mask of alcohol. The father I had always needed. Thanks DAD!

After that, I learned that my father loved his family in spite of his struggle with alcohol. He was certainly a provider for us. He worked all of the time doing various jobs, but most of his work was fixing automobiles. However, he could fix anything that had a motor. He was so good with his mechanical knowledge, he was the only black man that I knew that worked as a mechanic for Perish bus line in Bogalusa, I do not remember the name, but I think it was the Silver Eagle bus line.

13

It was a mystery to me why we did not have a car; after all, my Dad repaired everybody's car in the project. I know now that it was a blessing we did not have a car. Our family life was in less danger without a car, although Dad occasionally drove the cars that he repaired.

Our house was the local automotive repair shop. It seemed that people would call Dad when he was good and drunk to come and fix their cars. Maybe, he was that good, he could do it in his sleep at least this was what I was told. They called him, "R.T." That was the initials for Robert Turner. I remember the smell of alcohol and gasoline when Dad would come home.

He would sometimes take us boys Robert, Wayne, Kenneth and Richard to work with him, to help with the minor chores around the service stations where he worked. One day he caught us playing while we were supposed to be working. That was the last time that happened. He gave us the beating of a lifetime when we got home. When Dad would catch us in an act that was cause for a beating, he would always say, "Yes sir, Buddy!" I do not know how this related to what was going to happen to us because to me "Buddy" had a different meaning than what daddy meant.

There were times when Dad would try to impress us, by showing us how to do things. He used this instructional time to show us how much he knew. This made him feel good about himself. I remember my brothers and I went to work with Dad at the home of a wealthy white man across the state

14

line into the State of Mississippi, about 30 miles from Bogalusa. We had worked all day and it was getting dark. We had to empty several large barrels into a ravine that had thick brush along the hill which obscured the water below. My Dad got impatient with us because we were moving too slow and it was dark in the woods near the ravine. Dad was angry with us, so he said, "Wait until you get home. I guess I am going to teach y'all a lesson." In his haste, with his cigarette in his mouth, he grabbed and picked up the barrel to lift and empty the contents over the edge of the ravine.

It was so dark the only thing we could see was the light from his cigarette moving in his mouth, as he mumbled words in disgust. As he lifted the barrel to throw the contents over the embankment, he disappeared into the darkness. I heard tree limbs breaking and then a splash, it was my Dad rolling down the embankment. He had slipped and he rolled with the barrel down into the water.

We were afraid to call his name. We quietly called, "Daddy, O' Daddy! Are you all right?" We could not see anything down the dark hill.

We thought maybe he was hurt, we shouted a little louder, "Daddy, are you all right?" Still no answer; then we heard some movement. It must be Dad! But, he was not saying anything. Then out of the darkness we saw a light coming up the hill, it was the end of Dad's cigarette. I knew then that we were really going to get it when we got home.

It was hard to keep from laughing. Our Dad rolling down the hill in the dark and the only thing you see is a light making a circular motion. You know at the other end of that light is your father, proud and stubborn. Yes, it would be a hilarious scene for a sitcom, but we knew it was not a laughing matter to Dad. We did not let Dad see us laughing, because Dad's ego was hurt more than he was physically hurt, and Dad would have said, "I ain't trying to be funny."

We knew that Dad could exercise his pride of being a man only with his sons. We would not dare humiliate our father. He suffered enough humiliation every time he had to say, "Yes sir!" to the white boys that were younger than us. We never lost respect for our Dad. He was a Father who provided for his family.

Bishop John W. White, My former Pastor in Bogalusa

Chapter Three

BOGALUSA PEOPLE

ogalusa was no different from any other small town in the south during the sixties. Race relations in Bogalusa were no more unique than the relations between Jews and Palestinians. The whites lived in their area and the blacks lived in theirs. The whites were located in the center of city, which caused some logistic nightmares during the height of the civil rights struggle, because we had to pass through the white community to get to the, "colored" sections (this was what it was called by the natives) of Bogalusa. It was very dangerous for blacks to stop in the white part of town, unless they were going to work at one of homes of the privileged citizens of Bogalusa.

- Established in 1819, Washington Parish, Louisiana was formed from the northern half of St. Tammany Parish.
- Bogalusa was founded by the GOODYEARs (Frank Henry GOODYEAR and Charles Waterhouse GOODYEAR), William Henry SULLIVAN, and others who erected a

sawmill on the Bogue Lusa Creek where it
flows into the Pearl River in 1906.
- Bogalusa is the only incorporated city in
  Washington Parish, Louisiana. Incorporated
  in July 4, 1914. Franklinton is the County
  seat.
- Bogalusa is where the Great Southern
  Lumber Company Sawmill (1908 -1938),
  Bogalusa Paper Company (1918 -1937), New
  Orleans Great Northern Railroad and related
  ventures were undertaken.
- Bogalusa has been called the "Magic City "

When I mention the name Bogalusa for the
first time to someone unfamiliar with Louisiana
they think I am talking about a foreign country. The
next question is, "Where is that?" or "What city is it
by?"

Then I get into my mode of charades and
start gesturing with my hands trying to draw a boot
"You know, a boot that goes on the foot," I explain
that Louisiana is shaped like a boot and Bogalusa is
located right on the toe. With a puzzled look on
their faces, most people would say they got it.
Some would just give up keeping me from repeating
and going through the motions again; and I'd
quickly say, "OK, I know where it is, it is close to
New Orleans."

The downtown area was a narrow street
dotted with small stores and other businesses. In the
heart of the city stood the largest paper mill in the

South, with its towering smoke stacks billowing white smoke, suffocating the town with an aroma you could smell fifty miles away. This was home for the first seventeen years of my life.

Most of the people I grew up with in Bogalusa were friendly and polite. Even if you did not know the person, they would speak to you with a courteous smile, "Hi, there, how are you today?" It seemed like everybody that knew you, was concerned about your family. "Wayne, how is your Mama doing?" or "How is your Grandmother? I heard she was sick last week." Their concern seemed genuine.

Each family had a nickname. All of the Penton family was given the nickname, "Bull Dog." I do not have a clue how we got that name, but sometimes your friends or family members give you a personal nickname that describes a personal characteristic, such as "Bucket Head", "Squealer", 'Tweety,' or other nicknames that I will not

Sitting outside was a great past time for Bogalusa people.

The Church Drumer, Brother Tony & Niece

Tony Jacobs
Kindergarden –High
School Friend

mention in this book.

The people of Bogalusa were hard working people and the older people taught the younger people how to work. Most of the jobs were general labor jobs that required more muscles than brains. As long as you were an able body, there was always work.

There were seasonal jobs, like picking cotton. Yes, I picked cotton once! The reason it was only once was because the people did not want me to come back. I did not pick enough cotton to pay for the food I got on credit. It was a system they had, they knew most of the people could not afford to pay for their lunch, so they let them have all that they wanted on credit, at the little "mom and pop" store near the field. At the end of a workday, they would tally up what was owed and deduct that from the money you made for the amount of cotton you picked. Somehow I broke even. I came with no money and I left with no money. It did not take long to realize that these people "ain't trying to be funny."

Every community had its gathering place for old men to congregate and share their wisdom with each other, as they played a high intensity game of checkers.

William Spikes High
School friend

20

Charles Spikes High School friend

You could hear the sound of checkers hitting the board with the words, "Man, go ahead and crown me." Then you heard the cry, "Next!" This would go on for hours with the older men getting satisfaction from beating each other in a game of checkers. The younger men would play more active games such as tackle football without pads, tag baseball, which was also a contact sport the way we played. We usually made our balls with socks filled with old cloth material but around Christmas time we would have real balls to play with. We even played games that the girls could participate. The game of "Jacks" was often played with the girls.

When we got bored with one game, we created games and made rules as we went along. At night we gathered around the fire of burning rags as we told stories. The smoke from the burning

rags protected us from the mosquitoes. After story telling, we went inside to play a game of shooting down the flying "cockroaches" with our homemade "rubber band guns". These guns were made using the end of a broom handle, several rubber bands tied together with a paper clip on the end. The roaches never came out in the day. Night

21

was the time of the hunt. My brothers and I would get the rubber band guns ready then quickly turn the ights on and shoot. It was like shooting clay pigeons.

There are many stories that can be told about Bogalusa people, but I am only writing about a few of the experiences I remember. I hope you find them interesting. I enjoy sharing my story, the life story of a red black boy from a town named Bogalusa, Louisiana.

The most coveted job was working at the paper mill, everybody wanted to work at Zellar Back Paper Mill. It paid good money compared to the other jobs. The only other professional occupations the blacks could work were teachers or housecleaner (you know a more professional name would be maid).

We cannot forget the black entrepreneur, the Mom and Pop corner store that sold everything from a cup of sugar for 25-cents to two cigarettes for a dime. You did not have to buy a pack of anything. They just opened up a pack and down-sized it to fit your budget. The owner would ask me, "How much money you got, boy? Whatever the amount of money I had, they knew just how to make it work. This was a great system, it was before computers and calculators, but they knew how much 'a dollar's worth of anything' would be. If you did not have the cash they had a credit system. The old ledger would be taken down from the dusty shelf and opened. Then Mr. Smith would put his glasses on the edge of his nose, his face looking down at me while he went down a list to find the date and amount of our last payment.

The accounting was more accurate than the IRS. Mr. Smith would have the calculation of whatever you owed "down to the penny"; at least that was what he said and we did not question his figures. After all, we needed credit. Every time I was sent to the store with Mom's written list and without money, Mr. Smith would look in the book and read loudly what we owed and the last date we paid.

When we were late making payments, I was the messenger, "Mom, Mr. Smith wants his money."

We were always given a note with a list of items we were to get. I did not bother to look at the list. I just gave it to Mr. or Mrs. Smith and waited while the order was filled. I scouted the store to see what goodie I could get with the pennies I had in my pocket. "Those big wagon wheel cookies look very good!" I would say to myself, while Mr. Smith was checking off what was on the list. The hardest thing for me was trying to convince Mrs. Smith that Mom needed candy and cookies and pop for dinner. But never worked, Mr. Smith knew what we were allowed to buy on credit; cookies were not one of them.

"Mr. Fat Boy" was the owner of the community barbershop. His shop was not a place of democracy; it was dictatorship all the way. When you sat in Mr. Fat Boy's chair, you may as well close your eyes, take the pain, and the barber's choice of haircut. There was only one haircut style at Mr. Fat Boy's: the conventional bowl cut was the order of the day, every day. We could never ask him to just "take a little off the side and trim a little here." One cut fit all.

Mr. Fat Boy discovered a new hair cut by accident, the Nike swoop logo. He was trying to cut a straight part in my hair when I moved my head to avoid the painful dull manual clippers. It felt like he was doing brain surgery without anesthesia as he dug into my scalp to cut a "part" which ended up looking like the Nike "swoop." Back then, we called them "parts" and now Nike calls them swoops. It was not stylish then but it was different.

I wanted to know what was going on in the outside world, so I would go to the library and read the National Geographic magazine, the Readers' Digest, and occasionally I would find an Ebony magazine and look at the black folk I thought were from another planet. I would dream. I would see these good-looking people with their nice clothes and slicked down hair and say to myself that one day I wanted to be like that. In the Readers' Digest, I enjoyed the short stories and the jokes. This would give me hope. It was very important for me to see people like me doing things

Larry Lucas and Jimmy Brown High School Friends

24

that I hoped to do. It was also encouraging to go to school and see the successful black person, the teacher.In my family, Dad worked long hours as a mechanic, my mother worked as a maid and my grandmother worked as a maid. It got depressing, sometimes, to see your parents working long hours and still struggling to pay bills. Yet I knew they wanted the best for my sisters and brothers and me. Our family had limited exposure to the American Dream. Therefore I was a dreamer with the desire to become all that I could in the American dream.

John's Graduation
1967

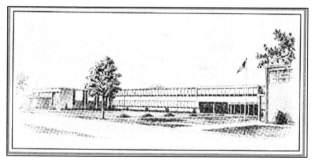

O' Central the place of the Spartan's

25

Chapter Four

DREAMER

I was always a dreamer. I would picture in my mind what I thought I wanted to be and then imagine that I was a cowboy, soldier or businessman. I would dress just like the people in the magazines that were in the profession I preferred at the moment. I remember finding an old brief case around the house, putting my grandfather's hat on my head and wearing by father's tie to school, looking like an old man in the ninth grade. I didn't have anything in the brief case, other than old books the school gave us. I just knew if I could look the part I would some day be a real businessperson. I did not know what business I wanted to be in, but business was business.

The first order of business was to leave Bogalusa. Bogalusa did not offer the opportunities I saw in Ebony magazine. I knew the principles of business: supply and demand. I learned this from my grandmother. My grandmother was a great example of a businessperson. She really knew the principle of supply and demand. She would take a 5-cent package of "Kool-ade", mix it, and make about twenty Dixie cups of "Kool-ade." Then she would freeze them and sell them for 5 cents each. What a mark up! She had customer service down better than Wal-Mart. Her charming smile would cool you off on a hot summer day and warm you when it was cold.

I remember a hurricane when the wind was blowing so hard that the garbage cans were being literally tossed through the air. To keep the wind from blowing the front door open, we had to use our heavy old piano to block the door closed. It was terrifying, but it did not stop the kids from going to Grandma for their Dixie cup treats. The gale was furious, and the kids held tightly to the doorknob to keep from being blown away. The tempest roared and drowned out the children's voices. However, we could read their lips, "One strawberry, and two pineapple frozen cups, please!"

My grandmother's entrepreneurial spirit must have passed on to me. I discovered in my junior year of high school that I could make money with a camera I had found. Actually, I took the liberty to use a camera left at my aunt's house by a man she was dating. I do not know why he left the camera and did not return to get it, but I knew it was something I wanted. I didn't know how to operate the camera, so I went to the local photography studio to ask if anyone knew how to operate the camera. It seemed they either did not want to take the time to show me or they did not know. I became determined to learn know how to operate this camera.

After playing with the camera for weeks, I bought film and just started shooting. To my surprise, the pictures came out. My entrepreneurial spirit flowed. I brought the camera to school. I figured if I charged one dollar per picture I could make a profit of 60% on each roll of film. I found out very quickly that most people like to see themselves in a photograph. Those that did not like to see themselves bought the pictures to keep others from seeing them. It was a good business until the principal, Mr. Crump, got word that I was making money on the school campus. Mr. Crump, a greatly respected man of short stature, caught me in the act of collecting payment. He told me the rules, and added I could not be on the school grounds. I quickly learned that the school grounds ended across the street. So I had my clients meet me across the street where taken pay me he sun as shining. My system was: if you wanted your picture you paid half now and the balance when the pictures were developed. It worked well until my senior year, when I was asked to take pictures at the senior party. I had never taken pictures at night or in a

rk setting. I knew I would need to brighten up the place to take the pictures. I didn't have any technical knowledge about photography. I just knew light makes the picture. I borrowed a large spotlight from one of the teachers. The problem was that the light was not a flash. I had to turn it on. When it was on it lit up the whole gym where the kids wanted a dimly lit atmosphere.

Every time, I would take a picture, I would hear the roar from the crowd, "Turn off the light." I

29

tried to turn the light on and off as quickly as possible to synchronize with the shutter. This took some coordination trying to make a spotlight into a flash. The clicking went on all though the party. thought the party. The flickering of the lights going on and off drew more attention to my operation in the corner. I got so busy in that corner I could not coordinate a system of writing names and matching names with the people I was photographing. Eventually, I lost the count and the names. However, I never lost count of the money. When the party was over, I had so many dollar bills in my pocket and as I was walking out with my hands on my money, someone reminded me that I had brought a girl, whom I did not dance or talk with at the party. A voice came from behind, "Hey Penton, you didn't even dance with your girl," I was so involved with my success of the night, I replied without turning around to see who was making the statement, I said, "Man, making money was more important than dancing or my girl."

Suddenly, I heard this high-pitched voice come out of the crowd behind me, I knew instantly it was she, the girl I forgot I brought. I really did not understand what she said, but knew what she meant. What I thought she said was, "Let me at him!"

I learned quickly how to talk someone out of killing me. This was just the beginning of my business woes. I had all these rolls of film and money without a list of the people I had photographed. I thought this would be easily solved when the pictures were developed.

After counting the money, I noticed most of the people had paid me in advanced. This was good until I went to the photo lab to pick up the pictures. Everybody had been asking me about their pictures because it had been several weeks since the party and graduation was coming soon. The man just looked at me as I came through the door of the lab, he did not need to say a word. I learned again that "life isn't lived by accident, or death spared by ignorance"

He spoke, "John, none of the pictures came out, because the light was not correct." It would have been better to have been hurt by my girlfriend that night of the party then I could have blamed her. Now my dilemma was compounded, I had spent the money and I did not know whose pictures I had taken. So I did not know who to avoid. I only knew if I could survive until graduation, I could at least die as a hero in Vietnam.

Graduation was a time of joy and sadness. It was sad because I was leaving friends that I had been with throughout my school years, from kindergarten to high school. My friend Tony G. Jacobs was my messenger to the girls I did not have the courage to talk to: Tony Jacobs always knew the right words to say. We took the same subjects, and we had a crush on the same female teacher. The only time we were not together was when I participated in sports. Tony was more interested in academics than sports. However, I had other friends that played sports, William Earl Spikes the baseball player. We became good friends. He and his brother Charles Spikes played Major League Baseball after High School. Charles played with several teams, Cleveland and the New York Yankees and William played with the Pirates.

I remember playing in the state championship game in my senior year of high school. I played centerfield and the Spikes boys were in left and right field. We played the championship game on the Grambling College Campus. It was Central Memorial High School Spartans from Bogalusa verses the High School from Shreveport, Louisiana. I do not remember the name of the school, but I remember one of the players named Vida Blue which became a legend with the Oakland A's. We won the game 1-0, with only one hit a home run! Charles Spikes hit it over the left field fence.

Many of the players were signing scholarships and contracts with Major League Teams. I did not have any offers for either a scholarship or a Major League contract, but I did sign up, The Navy!

Martin Luther King Dream came true, Bogalusa got their first Black Police Officer 1967 ?

Chapter Five

THE NAVY, THE WAY TO GO

Many of the young men during this time were being drafted into the army. It was 1967, a critical time during the Vietnam era. I knew when I graduated my chance of being drafted was very great. My parents did not have the money to send me to college. So I knew I would be going to the war. Since I had to go, at least I could choose the branch of service; I chose the Navy. My logic was very simple; I did not want to be in the jungle fighting. I felt that being on the ship was a little safer than being among snakes and insects.

I also joined the Navy to fulfill my dream of being a photographer. I discovered that I had a better chance of becoming a photographer since the Navy had a photography lab on board.

When I was recruited at the post office I was treated really nice by white people for the first time. They called me by my first name and I felt like a man. I remember the day we were scheduled to leave; flying to boot camp in California. The navy sent a limousine to pick us up from Bogalusa and carry us seventy miles to New Orleans. This was a trip of a lifetime. Here I was a boy whose family

never had a car; a boy who had never been in a vehicle with a white
person, I was now riding in a limo with seven white guys driving seventy miles in the seventh month "July" in 1967. I guess this was my lucky day.

I was on my way to Sunny California on an airplane for the first time. I must have looked frightened because as
I got on board I passed through the first class section going to the rear of the plane; and I got the attention of a black man that was seated in first class. After the plane had taken off, he asked me to come and sit in the empty seat next to him. I cannot remember his name but I knew he was a professional football player. I wish I could remember his name. He was so encouraging to me. He was one of those Ebony magazine people. He was just like the people I saw in Ebony magazine. Just by being with him took my mind off the fear of flying, and the purpose for which I was going to California.

I wore the tropical shirt that my Mom had given me; I was dressed for California, looking as if I was ready to go to a rich and famous retreat. My little bag was packed with what I thought people wore in California.

The plane landed in the darkness of the night.

E-3 Seaman Penton 1968

After we had deplaned and were standing on the curb, I heard this voice I had never heard before call out, "Those that are coming to navy boot camp form a line near the curb and stand at attention." I stood at attention with the precision of a well trained

Fresh out of boot camp company 428

military man. If "Gomer" could do it, I could too. The Gomer Pyle show was a popular TV show during my senior high school year.

I stood there for what seemed hours, until this large grey bus came out of the darkness and parked next to the curb. Out of the darkness the voice said, "Pick up your luggage and get on the bus."

As I was getting on this dimly lighted bus, I was looking out of the window trying to see at least one of those orange trees I had heard about. It was dark, I could not see anything. I just sat in my seat looking out at the blackness of the night wondering whether this was all real or was I in the "Twilight Light Zone."

We finally, arrived at this gated area. The gate slowly opened and the bus drove through. The closing clang of the gate was the ending to one chapter in my life and the beginning of another. I was really in the Navy!

When the sun came up the next day and I looked around: the color of the day was gray, the building, the vehicle, everything was gray. Whatever happened to sunny California? I did not get a chance to wear my stylish California shirt. The same old man that had me standing at attention the night before, told me to put everything I brought with me into a box he had placed at my feet and to put my home address on it.

He said, "You will not need these anymore, you are in the navy now." What did I get myself into? This was not part of the dream I had for myself. This was the nightmare part. Maybe I will wake up and start another day. After many tears in the nights and adjusting to the reality of being in the Navy, I became transformed from a little red country boy from Bogalusa to this new sailor with high expectations of fulfilling his dream of being a real photographer.

The Navy had various skills that they offered for those that qualified. Photography was my desire. We were

PH 3 Penton 1969

38

PH2 Penton 1969

told to fill out what was known as a dream sheet. It was called a dream sheet because you were asked to put down what your first choice would be; whether it was a boatswain mate or the more highly skilled jobs that the Navy offered. Naturally, I put down photography and then I chose an Aircraft Carrier as my duty station. An Aircraft Carrier was the only ship that had a photography lab on board. They gave me an aptitude test to determine what and where I would be for the next four years of my life.

The test revealed that I was more suited for clerical work or general labor. I was heart broken because I knew this was my best chance of being what I had always wanted to be, a photographer. The Navy gave me the white stripes to indicate my rating as a common sailor. In other words, you will do whatever they tell you to do. Shine the brass, mop the floor or should I say deck. I knew the test did not reflect my determination. I did what I was asked to do with the idea that one day I would be a Navy photographer.

It was all but wishful thinking to get

Sitting of the Dock

my rating changes after I had been assigned the white stripes E-2 Seaman. Here I was aboard ship with a rag to shine the brass and a mop to clean the floor. It did not require much thinking to do the jobs I was assigned, so I used most of my time thinking of how I could become a photographer even against the odds. During my off hours, I would go to the photo lab to ask questions about becoming a photographer. I told them I would volunteer my off time to work
around the lab just to become more knowledgeable about navy photography.

They would not let me come behind the counter at the lab because the security classification the photographers had was different from the white stripers' seamen. The photographers were kind enough to let me come down and talk with them. I know they were tired of seeing my face every day. I did find out that the only way I could ever become a photographer, was that I had to have a person trade from the Photographers' Lab to become a seaman. This would require a miracle. Who would change from the gravy job of photographer to become a brass cleaner and floor sweeper, or should I say from the elite to the delete? Yes, my job as a seaman was essential to the success of the ship's mission, but it was not essential in my personal strategy of fulfilling my dream.

I can fly..

I noticed that I was faced with a challenge that seemed impossible, which made me more determined to overcome. Here I am faced with a situation that was just right for prayer. I had a praying mother who taught me to pray in times of difficulty, and I knew that everything would be all right after prayer. In my heart I believed that God somehow would make a way for me. I never prayed that someone would trade with me, because I knew no one would do that. I prayed to be a photographer. I didn't know how God would do it, but really felt that he would. Months passed, and I kept going to the lab.

One day I was leaving the lab with no expectations then I heard a voice behind me saying, "Penton, we are going to get you down here." I did not see who was saying this, so I thought someone was playing a joke on me because after many months it was public knowledge that I wanted to be a photographer. I turned around suddenly and with irritation I made a comment that suggested doubt.

When I turned, I noticed that the person talking was the Warrant Officer in charge of the lab. I felt like Mary must have felt when the angel told her that that she had been chosen to be the mother

Looking at photos from lab

of Jesus. My reply was the same, "How could this be?"

He told me that he knew a person that wanted to be traded. I thought I would be happy to hear this, but I was not. A trade meant that someone would be traded and placed in the position I was in. I did not think there was anyone who would want to do what I was doing. I asked who the person was so I could talk with him personally. I wanted to hear from him. I met the person, his first name was Clark, I do not remember his last name. He told me that he wanted out of the navy. When he expressed this to his superior he became a security risk and no longer could work as a photographer.

God had placed a ram in the bush. Clark and I went through the official process of signing the papers required for the exchange. My white stripes were now green, just what I wanted: the rating of aviation seaman. This rating was the entry level of becoming a photographer's mate.

Now I was able to officially work in the photo lab and have my security clearance upgraded the same as the photographers. I found out shortly after the trade was made, Clark was discharged from the Navy. Yes, God worked it out. The trade with Clark was like God placing the ram in the bush. Clark would have been discharged from the

a real six pack, smile!

Navy even if the trade had not taken place, because his tour was near the end.

When I was first assigned to the lab one the photographers gave me the tour of the lab. I could tell by his sarcastic remarks he didn't want me as a part of the elite. When we got to the sink, he said, "Penton, this is how you mix water," as he turned the faucet on to emphasize how ignorant I was in the lab.

He was correct I was ignorant. However, this made me more determined to excel. I became his superior in less than two years. I went from aviation seaman E-2 and excelled to Photographers Mate E-5. I was 19 years old. It was kind of nice to have those guys who did not think I was going to amount to anything see the stripes on my shoulder as I paraded through the ship. Those stripes reminded them that I was the man who had accomplished the goal of becoming a photographer's mate.

I was a walking testimony that had the favor of God, and I knew it. I had become a household word around the ship. I mentioned God so much in my journey to promotion, I became known as the "Preacher." It is amazing how it came so natural to give God the credit for the direction my life was taking toward fulfilling the desires of my heart. I knew it was by providence that I was in this position. I could not boast about the formal training I had in photography because I had not received any formal training in the Navy or as a civilian. I came in the navy fresh from high school. The only knowledge I had about photography is what I learned by experimenting with the camera I had in high school.

I knew in order to advance and get a permanent rating of photographer's mate I had to pass the military's photography test. This test consists of the technical and practical knowledge of photography. I found a photographer's study manual and read as much as I could. When the test was given, I was ready as I could be with the knowledge I received from the manual. There were other factors I had to consider, besides passing the test. The Navy, over all, had to have a need for another photographer. Photography was a very popular rate in the Navy; therefore the selection process was arduous.

The result of the test was posted weeks later. The names were

Film getting tangle

posted in a public area aboard ship. All that were interested could see the list. I needed courage to go look at the list, because I could not bare it if my name was not there. It was a great relief when I saw my name in black and white. "John Wayne Penton, Bogalusa, Louisiana: Passed." What a great feeling, here I was standing among the men who had done well in the test, men who had training from some of the best technical schools. My professional photography career had just begun.

The hard part had just begun. I must now actually do photography. I had many bloopers in the beginning. I remember one of my first assignments as a photographer was to go to the Admiral's cabin to photograph some public relations photo for a presentation. I was so nervous that I came down to develop the film and found that I did not have film in the camera. On another occasion I had to shoot a cake-cutting ceremony celebrating some successful pilot bombing over Vietnam. The camera was one of those large "Crown Graphic" cameras with accordion-pleated bellows. In order to focus, the bellow had to be secured by a stop located on the track. I didn't know this, I had pulled the bellow out well beyond the stop. I was wondering why the lens of the camera was on top of the cake frosting. The cake was eaten up before I could

Standing by jet on flight deck

45

get a retake.

Once I asked the Captain if he could do a hand shake again, because I missed it. He got angry and said "I suppose you want us to do the war over again so that you can get a picture." As time went on I got better. I practiced until I knew how to quickly shoot and anticipate the action of the activity I was to shoot.

When I got better, I was assigned to more serious photographic tasks. One task was to photograph the planes on the flight deck as they took off and returned from their bombing runs. This was very challenging because it was very dangerous. I had to be aware of the jets engines that could blow me off the ship or suck me into the engine intake. One sailor had this happen to him and it was a terrible sight to photograph. I remember I had to develop the photos of this person's badly mangled body in the darkroom. It was kind of spooky, seeing grisly photos slowly come out in the darkroom under the special darkroom light. That was the quickest developing job I ever did.

The adventures I had in the Navy were foundational to the journey ahead. Being at Sea on the USS Ranger CVA-61, I was constantly faced with potential life threatening predicaments. I had to be alert at all times. The minute

John taking college courses

I let my mind drift from the task at hand, I was in imminent danger. It took an angel working overtime to keep me from injury and death.

Billy Graham preaching aboard Ship *Billy Graham talking with Captain*

Billy Graham talking with Sailors

Chapter Six

DANGER, THE HIGH JUMP

The Sea was rough during a routine cargo exchange with a supply ship. When the exchange is done at sea each ship rigs large steel cables on pulleys that are attached to a secure area on each ship; the cargo is attached to the cable and then carried across to the other ship. When we were in turbulent seas the ships moved up and down creating a "roller coaster" motion, which caused the cables to slack and sometimes drag on the deck. It is very dangerous when the cables are slacking and dragging across the deck, because in a split second the motion of the sea can create tension in the cables.

The hangar deck was below the flight deck. The elevator carried the planes from the hangar deck to the flight deck. The elevator is lowered during the supply exchange operation. My position was on the hangar deck elevator. I almost became another statistic during a supply exchange at sea. I was caught on the outer area of the elevator that takes the planes up. The cable was dragging on the deck and I thought it would be safe to walk over the cable. Wrong! When I raised my feet to make the step, the ship responded to the shifting seas and the tension caused the cable to pull up about seven feet. I heard someone scream and then shouting words only a boatswain mate could say. I jumped straight up as if someone had grabbed me under my arms and lifted me. The cable moved like a sling-shot and could have cut me in half, killing me instantly.

My heart was pounding so hard that I thought everyone around me could hear the rapid beating. I knew God had protected me. When I looked at the height of the cable after I was moved to safety, it was apparent that God gave me the strength to jump as high as I did.

There were other sailors who had life threatening experiences and lived to tell their story. But Rodgers did not live to tell his story. He was lost at Sea.

Inr rough seas 1

Chapter Seven

LOST AT SEA

The ocean had multiple personalities, some times it would be as calm as a spring day with a refreshing breeze, its surface as smooth as glass reflecting light from the sun at day and the moon at night. Then, there was the raging sea with giant waves tossing the 55,000 ton ship frantically like an angry child playing with a toy boat in the bathtub. The sea was always a dangerous place, yet it had its beauty. As I lay in my cubicle, sometimes the rolling of the waves would rock me to sleep, just as my mother rocked me to sleep when I was a child. The sound of the waves rising and falling against the hull of the ship would at times be as soft as the singing of a lullaby

Yet, this beauty can take a life seemingly without remorse. On December 7, 1969 the sea swallowed a young man, I only knew as Rodgers. He was an African American from the east coast. We had met briefly while coming back to the ship from a beach in the Philippines. Even though we were on the same ship this was our first meeting. The ship had over 5,000 men on board and they were scattered all over the ship, which made it hard to get to know everybody. It was not surprising to meet people for the first time even though they had been aboard ship for months.

We quickly became friends and shared our future plans beyond the navy. He would tell me with a smile on his face about the girl he was going to marry. I shared with him some of my dreams. After the ship left the dock, the chance of meeting Rodgers again was slim, unless I knew where he bunked.

The ship left port and was out at sea for days, when suddenly the ship make an unexpected turn, and the captain came over the speaker system, "Man overboard! Man overboard! All men go to your 'man overboard' station." The countdown began, as all the men aboard were running to take

USS Ranger CVA-61 during cargo exchange

their positions. Some men ran to small boats and helicopters to search in the water for the man overboard. Everyone had to go to their assigned stations and be counted to determine who went overboard.

All men on board had to be accounted for within three minutes. These three minutes seemed like hours, while we waited for the captain to speak the name of the person lost at sea. After I was accounted for, I went to a room in the photo lab to be alone, so I could pray. As I was praying the captain came over the speaker and said with a sad voice, "Lost at sea, Rodgers....."

I said to myself, "Rodgers, I just had talked with him before we left port." I could not understand how God could let this happen to a man that was so happy and full of life.

The Captain said, "Let's have a moment of silence for our brother lost at sea." Then the bugle played "Taps" and it was over. All this took place within five minutes total. The subtle reality was that the ocean with its poetic grandeur had become the final tomb of a friend in a matter of minutes.

It was known that if a person could not be found within several minutes of being in the water, he would be dead. My mind, rehearsed what he and I had talked about. I tried to remember if I had talked with him about Jesus. I knew I usually talked with the men I met about salvation. I am not sure if I talked with him about Christ during our brief time together, I assumed he was a Christian. I knew I had invited him to the Bible study we had aboard ship during the week. Of course, he did not get a chance to come. I wanted very much to believe He was with the master Teacher, Jesus Christ.

The USS Ranger was a floating City with 5,000 citizens with the same problems as the cities of the country it was protecting: Race Relations. The news about the civil rights struggle from the homeland would sometimes make emotions run high, and cause a strain on race relations. The Navy would try to address the problem by having town meetings aboard ship to talk openly about the subject. There were times when the Navy would invite civilians to come on board and act as mediators between the Blacks and Whites.

I found myself in the role of peacemaker. Many years before Rodney King, I said, "Can't we all get along?" I knew too well, the reality of segregation. I needed to see a miracle, a real life example of men coming together without hostile intentions.

Barry M. Goldwater once said, "When white and black and brown and every other color decide they're going to live together as Christians, then and only then are we going to see an end to these troubles."

"These troubles" were opportunities to make a friend or foe.

Chapter Eight

FRIEND OR FOE

I made a few enemies being zealous about my belief in Christ, but most people knew I was sharing something that was dear to me. I guess you can say, I was "OJT"– on the job training. I enjoyed sharing the good news. It was good news to me, but for some it was not good news. The sailors that were not receptive to the message of Salvation let me know by avoiding me when they saw me from a distance. The ship was large and had many places to hide; however, the port and starboard passageways were narrow. It was difficult to avoid me in those narrow passageways. I would strategically position myself in the passageway so that I could run into the unsuspecting sailor. I would not just come right out preaching, I would disarm them and talk about current events and things that I knew would interest them. I was so smooth they did not know they were being set up, I knew how to bait the hook. It was like fishing in a barrel.

We were out at sea off the coast of Vietnam, which was a distance away from inland where the soldiers were in

Black Sailors Sharing concerns about race relation

direct contact with the enemy. We would see fighter jets occasionally return to the ship with bullet holes reminding us we were in the war. We had to remember that we were at war with the North Vietnamese, not each other. When we realized that the uncertain environment we were in could easily take our lives, we got along better as sailors. The war in Vietnam was definitely an uncertain environment. Yes, we were at sea and away from the jungles, but the danger of losing our lives still existed.

"General quarters, general quarters!" meant, "Man your general quarters' station!" This was blasted over the speaker by the captain. This meant: stop whatever you were doing and get to your stations. The ship was as long as three football fields and as high as a 10-story building. We had three minutes to get to our stations. Each sailor had a station with a special assignment for each battle situation. For example, the "man over station", battle station, and fire station were all different. We had to know our various stations. We were constantly having drills for various situations. It became part of the daily routine to have a drill at different times of the day, just to keep us alert.

"General quarters, general quarters, all men man your battle stations!" roared the captain.

I ran to my station. My assignment was to watch a bomb to make sure it did not overheat. I was to hose it down if I saw any sign of smoke coming from the bomb. There was another sailor assigned to the same station. We were given instructions,

I asked, "What will happen if the water doesn't cool the bomb?

The chief petty officer gave me a sarcastic look and said, "Don't worry about it, you won't know anything."

I understood him very well. Here we are standing over this bomb just looking at it. It was a boring task, but someone had to do it. I had never met my newly assigned partner. We asked each other where we were from; to my surprise, he was

A break in the Photo Lab at Sea

from Bogalusa, Louisiana, too. What were the chances of two Bogalusa's being in the middle of the ocean, thousands of miles away from home? I knew I did not know him from home because he was white

57

and I had never gone to school with any one that was white. He was friendly enough as we talked. We shared our names. I remembered his family name, because my mother worked for a family with that name in Bogalusa. He was somehow related to this family which was known to be affiliated with the KKK in Bogalusa. Imagine for a moment how I felt; standing over what I thought was a nuclear bomb with this person I knew had ties with the KKK. However, at this point we were on the same team with one goal in mind, to stay alive.

Standing over a bomb was an ideal setting to talk with him about heaven or hell. I had his complete attention. When I invited him to our Bible Study, he wanted to go right then, but we had this matter of watching a bomb. Needless to say the bomb did not go off. He did come to our next Bible Study and accepted Christ as his Savior. He was very excited about his new change of life. I had never seen a white person dance in the spirit until then. Here was this person with experiences of burning crosses as a symbol of hate, who now had a cross burning in his heart as a symbol of love. I was beginning to understand that the changing of a man's heart was the greatest of all miracles. My faith in humanity was bolstered. We were from different backgrounds, yet we had so much in common. We kept in contact while at sea.

Bob Hope entertaining about ship in Vietnam

Yes, "Join The Navy To See The World" at least that is what I heard from the navy commercials. I had sailed the Pacific Ocean several times, completing several Vietnam tours aboard the same ship the "USS Ranger CVA-61. This was my cruise line for three years, three months and twenty-seven days. During this time, I took time to meet people from the various countries we visited. Japan and the Philippines were our most frequent ports visited. We would pull in these ports after months out at sea. This was time for the men to go on liberty to have fun.

I tried to experience the infamous sailor life; sometimes I went with the sailors to the bars to see what the nightlife was all about. I was not impressed, the smoked filled rooms, the smell of alcohol and the loud sound of the music did not seduce me; but I did find myself interested in the girls. I was afraid to drink too much. I knew that if I started drinking it would be difficult to stop. My Dad was my example. Therefore, my conscience did not let me drift too far. I put on a show, by putting Listerine on my breath and acting as if I was drunk. It was interesting to see what people do under the influence of the alcohol.

Fighting was common during the late hours when out on the town. I never got into a fight, but I stopped a few after returning late to the ship. I tried the nightlife and I would come back to the ship feeling that I had let myself down. This was not the life I was accustomed too. I prayed in my 2'x 6'cubicle until I felt refreshed. Thank God for other Christian sailors aboard ship. We needed each other for support. I met Dudley, he worked in flight operations. I was surprised to see this rather tall African American sailor sporting a "flat top" hair cut. Dudley's personality radiated joy and cheer. We hit it off immediately. I looked to him when I was in need of encouragement. It was hard sometimes trying to be this strong Christian all alone, I needed fellowship. Our faith in Christ really bonded us. Now I had someone to pray with. Our friendship turned into a ministering team, we began to witness and other sailors came to know the Lord.

Our group had gotten to be very popular aboard ship or should I say we were infamous. A large portion of the ship's population did not want to hear the message we were sharing and others who only wanted us to pray for them when they were in trouble. The word was out that "a revival" was taking place in various compartments aboard ship. Our Bible studies had many sailors pass through and they were telling others. The chaplain on board was not very fond of our group, because he did not consider us a mainstream Christian group. Our group was a combination of various denominations, but we were Pentecostal in our

60

worship and expression of our faith. This really didn't set well with the chaplain. However, he could not deny the power of God was getting the attention of the sailors. He tried to discourage us from using the chapel which would hold about 50 sailors, but we knew that he could not stop us because it was our right as sailors. We knew we could practice our Christian faith.

We were so popular that the local ship's armed forces radio stations asked me to broadcast on Sunday. This was great because the station could be heard all over the ship. What an opportunity to reach sailors. I would preach sermons about adultery when the ship would be near port and the sailors were waiting to go ashore. You can imagine the attention it got. I am sure if they could turn the station off, they would have. I was notorious for my routine tour of the sick bay where the sailors would be standing in line waiting to get their shots for the sexual disease they contracted while on "liberty." I knew my presence would embarrass some, and be a reminder to them of the sermons I had preached prior to going into port. There was one sailor standing in line with a smile on his face as if he was going to pick up a lottery check. I was surprised for a moment, until I found out he was a virgin before, he considered his first sex experience as confirmation he was a man, he was proud to be in the line. He was not a candidate for repentance. The Navy tried to discourage the sailors from engaging in "unsafe" sex by showing gross films to the sailors of men that had contracted various sexual diseases it did not stop the sailors from taking the risk.

When we were in port, barhopping was the common pass time for many of the sailors. I found pleasure in meeting the natives of the countries we visited. The Philippines was my favorite country. The people were very friendly. I had a promise, I had to keep in the Philippines; I was to locate a family that was related to a friend from Bogalusa. It took a miracle to fulfill this promise.

Chapter Nine

THE MIRACLE IN THE PHILIPINES

After each tour overseas, I took 30 days leave and returned to my hometown, Bogalusa. While home, I learned that the brother of a first grade schoolmate was killed in June of 1967, while serving with the army in Vietnam. I knew the family. The father was an African American and the mother was Filipino. They had met during World War II when he was stationed with the army in the Philippines. They married and move to Bogalusa. Their children were beautiful, especially their daughters; one of whom I had a crush on in elementary school. I found out that her mother had sisters and brothers who were still in the Philippines; she had not seen them since World War II. This was my chance to impress this special girl from the first grade. I made a promise to the Johnson family that when I went back to the Philippines I would locate their family in the Philippines. I really did not know where to begin.

Johnson Family in the Philipines

This was my chance to be a humanitarian and at the same time make an impression the girl I had dated secretly in my mind as a child. Our ship left port from Alameda, California going on a "West Pac" cruise. The ship was scheduled to dock in the Philippines in December 1969. I needed much useful information about the area in the Philippines where I was told the people lived. The Filipino sailors aboard ship were very helpful to me. They gave me names of people they knew could help me get to the northern part of the Luzon province. Mrs. Johnson had given the name and the address in the Luzon Province where her family was known to have stayed. She was not certain if her family would still be there, it had been since World War II she had been back to her homeland. I mailed a letter with my photo to this address. The address did not appear to be complete. However, when I showed it to the Filipino sailor that had relatives in Luzon province, He knew the area, but he was not familiar with the name. He offered

Child standing by jeep

his services to connect me with people that provided transportation for me to the Luzon Province.

The ship docked at the United States Naval Base in Olongapo Philippines for R & R, I asked permission from my superiors, to take a trip to the northern part of Luzon which was about 400 mile from the Olongapo. It was in an area of the Philippines that was not registered as a place where American sailors were allowed normally to go. I was determined to succeed with my mission. I really believed God would help me. Ruiz was the

The people that traveled with me

Filipino sailor who was very helpful. He was a native of the Luzon Province. He provided me with transportation, drivers, and interpreters, all for 20 dollars. The transportation was a jeep-like vehicle with the capacity to hold six people comfortably.

I needed a camera, a tape-recorder and clothes that would endure the week journey in the jungle area of northern Luzon. Ruiz knew I needed something else, cigarettes. He mentioned I should buy a carton of cigarettes.

Climbing for Coconuts

I asked, "Why do I need cigarettes when I don't smoke?"

He said, "Just buy them we will need them." I did not know the cigarettes were going to be given to the soldiers we met along the way through various check points miles away from the Naval Base.

The first check point was at the gate of the US Naval Base in Olongapo. I remember going through the security check at the gate. I was stopped and searched. I knew that security was looking for contraband. One item they had labeled contraband was portable tape recorders. A portable tape recorder was the main item I needed to accomplish my mission. However, I took a chance because the mission required

Fresh coconut Milk

66

that I tape the voices to the family when I found them. I saw Security taking things out of my bag, looking as if they knew I had contraband. I had packaged the small tape recorder in a cover that looked just like a Bible. They looked at it while I was sweating hoping they would not open it. I was relieved when they put it back in my baggage without opening it and then motioned me to go through. As I was walking forward with a sigh of relief, the security officer gestured that I return to the check point.

When I returned, he said, "What is that you have in your hand?"

I was not sure what he was referring to, because I only had a ballpoint pen in my hand. I knew it was all over, they got me! When I got closer, he reached out to take the pen from my hand,

Power to the people!

and said, "You can't take government property across the security check point." He saw the writing on the pen had an inscription 'government property'.

I almost laughed in relief because I thought he was calling me back to get the tape recorder. I held my composure; I did not want my bags to be rechecked. I was so glad to give up a pen. This was the beginning of a four-day journey

Sitting in the shade with the Johnsons

Mr. Ruiz, two translators and I started from Olongapo. I was dressed in jeans. with my straw hat and backpack, ready to explore areas of the Philippines that would take me 400 miles through various villages and jungle areas. We stopped in villages to eat and visit some of the relatives of Mr. Ruiz. We stayed overnight in some of the villages, where the people graciously gave us their own bed. I insisted that they did not have to do this, but they said that they would be insulted if I did not take their bed. Their bed was a crude slab of wood covered with straw. Before going to bed we would talk around the fire with the smell of freshly ground coffee, I shared with them the purpose of my journey. The people that gathered around the fire were so receptive and supportive of the mission, they wanted to join us and take the journey with us. The jeep was too small to take everybody that wanted to go, but we allowed as many as would fit on the back of the jeep. I was surprised to see the excitement of these beautiful people crowding themselves in the jeep to travel with us. We got this response from the people in several of the villages we visited. After several days into the journey, we had about twelve people join us.

The Village where the Johnsons lives

The farther we traveled away from the military base the less the people were familiar with Americans and especially African Americans. One village where we stopped to eat and refuel, I decided to venture out on my own around the market place. To my surprise, I became the focus of attention at the market place. One man approached obviously staring at me and I was trying to ignore him. I did not want to bring more attention to myself, so I tried to look away. He walked around me, like someone would walk around a car to inspect it for any flaws. The man finally asked in fluent English, "Is it true that all American Negroes are from Texas?"

I responded trying to hold back laughter, "There are a lot of them in Texas." I gave a quick demographic lesson of the fifty states in the United States. I knew he was not trying to be funny, he was serious. He quietly walked away seeming satisfied with my answer.

I decided it was best that I return to my convoy. When I joined the rest of my convoy, I wanted to tell them of my experience in the market place, but I knew they would not understand. I was a novelty in the Philippines as an African American.

As we continued on our journey, I developed a fever and started to have chills in the 90-degree heat. I was getting sick and I needed to rest. They encouraged me to rest in a hut built in a tree. It was midday and the blazing sun's heat was bearing down on us, I did not have the energy to go on. I fell asleep protected from the sun in the shade of the hut. As I woke up and slowly opened my eyes, I noticed I had attracted an audience of the locals standing around me touching my hair and touching my skin as if I was the first black person

Boat on China Sea Beach

they had ever seen. It was fun explaining to them why my hair was the texture it was, and the color of my skin the same as theirs. I was the village celebrity, they loved me. I was accepted as a copper tone brother with a different type of hair.

It was morning when we finally arrived in the northern province of Luzon. We were riding on a road that bordered the China Sea on the left and

70

jungle on the right with a distant view of a mountain range. At that time of the morning there were very few people on the road. Mr. Ruiz saw a man riding in a donkey-drawn cart coming toward us on the dusty road. When he stopped him and asked if he knew the people we were looking for, the man appeared uncertain of the information and pointed toward the mountain range, which was about fifty miles away. This was disturbing because by this time my sickness had worsened. I could not stand without leaning on the side of the jeep for support.

When Mr. Ruiz came back to tell us that we had to go deeper into the jungle near the mountain, everyone got back into the jeep. As the driver turned the key, the engine coughed, sputtered and went silent. He kept trying to start the engine without success. Then Mr. Ruiz asked everyone to get off the jeep and push it to help start it. As I was leaning, trying to push along with the others, I prayed a simple prayer "Lord you know what I am trying to do, help us."

The jeep did not start. Therefore, several of the people went down the road in search of help. I stayed back because I was

too weak. While *Child eating*

the others were gone, we still tried to start the jeep. Twenty minutes later we heard the excitement of

Congregation of a church in northern Lozon

those who went for help. They had gone off the
road into a wooded area. We could not see clearly
from where we were but they were apparently
excited and were gesturing for us to come and see.
The way they were carrying on, I thought they had
found a pot of gold in the jungle or they were being
chased by some wild animal.

I moved slowly toward the animation. They
were speaking in their dialect. I only knew they
were excited about something. When I arrived, I
saw the reason for all the excitement. It was a
village and people. After they stopped speaking in
their dialect, I was told that the people we were
looking for lived in this village. I said, "Look at
God!" God knew where the people were. He had
the jeep stop no more than 100 yards from the
village. This was as profound to me as it was for
Balaam when the donkey he was riding decided to
stop and go no farther because of impending
danger. However, Balaam did not know it was

72

God's intervention on his behalf. The jeep was not a living beast, but I believe it was God's intervention that caused the jeep not to start.

I knew it was God because the jeep started 15 minutes after we discovered the people in the village. There was even more confirmation that the providence of God was involved: the letter with my photo had been delivered shortly before we arrived. The people were in awe, I was also in awe. My faith was strengthened. I almost forgot I was sick. They wanted to celebrate, so some of the young men in the village climbed up a coconut tree to get a fresh coconut and we drank fresh coconut milk. They gathered around to hear the story. The excitement took wing around the village, I felt like General Macarthur, "I have returned."

I was a hero for that moment. It was a great feeling of accomplishment. I photographed and taped the family. I wanted to get back to the ship to process the film and prepare a package to send to the United States for the Johnson family in Bogalusa, Louisiana.

After four remarkable miracle days, the journey back to the ship was not as exciting; I laid quietly in the back of the jeep all the way back on the long journey to Olongapo. When I returned to the ship, they admitted me to sickbay. The next day I was not sick. I could not figure out why I got sick during the trip and got well after the trip. The only conclusion was that God was helping me to avoid the temptation of getting side tracked by the beautiful Filipino women I met along the way to the

Luzon province. I guess God put a thorn in my side so that I would not be tempted above measure. It was very clear that God made me weak so that He could be strong. I am telling you, I was in the midst of paradise. Here I am in a tropical setting with some of the most beautiful girls. During the warm nights and clear skies, I could hear in the distance the strings of an acoustic guitar playing love melodies. Hey, man! I was sick, but I was not dead. These women reminded me of the girl I had a crush on in Bogalusa. I was too weak to do anything that my mind was suggesting. But I would not dwell on the potential distraction too long, I was on a mission.

When I returned to America, my priority was to visit the Johnson Family in Bogalusa. I was a hero to the Johnson family. Mrs. Johnson adopted me as her son. It was thrilling to watch some members of the family a seeing and hearing their relatives for the first time. Delighted, I observed the joy on Mrs. Johnson's face as she saw the pictures and heard the voice of her sister whom she had not seen since World War II. I admit my motive was a bit selfish, but it brought great happiness to the Johnson family. I knew this gave me some brownie points with their daughter. We never dated as girl and boy friends. She never indicated she even liked me in the same way. I guess when you are a young boy and a girl smiles at you, you think you are in love. I was the "Lone Ranger" that saved the day. As I left the family with joy and excitement, I faded into the shadows of obscurity. I had done something that brought joy to others. What a feeling!

It was near the final year in the Navy when I realized that I needed a wife to help me continue my journey through life. The hunt began, for the woman of my life.

The children having fun with the victory sign

Chapter Ten

THE WOMAN OF MY LIFE

Edmund Burke once said, "A woman is not made to be the admiration of all, but the happiness of one." Although Linda had the qualities of the virtuous woman she also had the charm of princess; these were the characteristics I was looking for in the woman I would marry.

My four years of military life was ending, I had to think about my future. I would read about career opportunities in the civilian world as we called it. I knew I had skills in the area of photography. Therefore, I felt secure about my working career. However, I was not so sure about my social career, I was lonely. I was not one of those sailors that had a woman in every port. I was looking for a woman in every port with that certain quality, that made me want to go to the trouble of dating. I met many possible candidates as I traveled in the Navy, but no one was as compelling as my interest in Linda.

Linda in the park

The USS Ranger was scheduled for repair that took

77

Linda in 1980

us to Bremerton, Washington. During this time in port, I met the Kinlows. I went to the first Church of God in Christ in the State of Washington. The Pastor was Nathaniel Kinlow, Sr. He had children my age and they treated me just like family. It was good finding a wonderful family while I was so far away from my home in Bogalusa, Louisiana.

I was treated like a brother in the Kinlow family. They took me under their wings, feeding me and picking me up for church. I thank God for the time I had with the Kinlows in Bremerton, Washington. Through the friendship of the Kinlow family, I met future friends as we visited other churches at district meetings.

One hot summer day we visited Tolliver Temple, a small church in Seattle, Washington, I was in the Spirit on the Lord's Day. I was in the balcony of the church and out of the corner of my eyes in the lower section I saw a girl that I just had to get to know. I could not see her face from the balcony because her hat was obstructing my view. I was trying to see something that would give me a reason to want to see more of her before I introduced myself. My eye fell

Linda baby picture, what a beauty

78

on her legs. I could not see very clearly, but I saw enough to know I wanted to see more. After the service, I introduced myself. Here, I was in my sailor uniform, looking like the sailor on the Cracker Jack box. I was a little nervous and she was shy. When I saw her face and that shy smile, something was going on inside me that let me know this was *the* girl. She did not give any indication that she was interested in me a serious way.

We exchanged information. I would call her and her sweet, high-pitched voice got me excited, but Linda was not very talkative during telephone conversations. However, when she did speak, she spoke very fast, sometimes I thought she was speaking in a foreign language. She did not talk like any other girl I had met. I had to keep saying something to get her to talk. Even though
there were dead spots of silence on the phone, just to know that she was on the other end made me feel good. Most of the time I initiated the conversation because I never took her silence on the other *Linda High School Picture 1* end as an indication she did not want to talk with me. Somehow, I knew she was getting to be more interested in me. I knew I was falling in love. I was hoping the ship did not leave Bremerton too soon. I knew I had to move with the ship.

My ship was scheduled to leave Bremerton after several months of minor repair. My life had

79

been changed. I was in love! I knew that the ship would be in the Alameda, California several months before we would deploy on another West Pac cruise. I kept in contact with my newly found joy. The telephone was my constant companion. I just had to hear that high-pitched sweet voice saying, "Hi, this is me, Linda." After those five words my heart would increase in tempo, I would say as Stevie Wonder says in his song, "I just called to say that I love you and that I care." Our conversations did not last long, but they had a lasting effect.

I just had to see this girl again. I had used all my leave time for the year. Our ship was leaving to go over seas. What was I going to do? What is 1300 miles when you are in love? I thought. I knew I had the weekend to leave ship, but could I travel 1300 to see my girl and be back in time at 6:00 AM for

Linda dressed and ready to go

muster Monday morning? All these questions were answered with an affirmative, yes, yes and yes! My next challenge was: where was I going to get the money to buy an airline ticket? The bus would have been too slow. I was only making seaman wages of ninety dollars a month. I never could afford a round trip. I would buy the one way ticket and hope I would get the money for my return trip either by shooting pictures or by getting a little here and there from friends and relatives I knew in the area.

My brother Bob and his wife lived in Tacoma not too far from Linda and they sometimes gave me money. Somehow, when Sunday night came I would have enough money to get a ticket to return to the Bay area in California. It is amazing what love does to people. The other travel challenge was cab fare from the airport to the ship when I arrived back to California. The trip from the airport to mass transit (the connecting bus I had to take to the ship) was over twenty miles.

The public bus transportation was not running at 4:00 AM from San Francisco to Oakland. I had to take a taxi to the connecting bus to get to my ship before 6:00 AM. I usually would have just enough money for the transportation from the airport to the ship. However, this time I did not have enough taxi fare. I kept walking around the airport in hopes that I would meet someone going my way. The airport looked like a graveyard at 4:00 AM. As I walked outside the door onto the "pick up" ramp, a cab drove up and the driver said in a hurried voice, "Get in."

I was trying to tell him that I did not have enough money, but he insisted that I get in. He drove off as I was trying to explain. I am sure he thought he had a sailor he could take advantage of because at that hour he knew I was desperate.

He said, "Where are you going?" I wanted to say where ever 75 cents would take me. I had

81

only 75 cents. I knew the fare would cost about 20 dollars. I had taken this route many times since Linda and I were separated by several States. We had driven away from the airport by the time he realized I was seriously broke. He said, with a voice of disappointment, "Give me what you got."

Embarrassed, I reached in my pocket and gave him my 75 cents and he looked at it with disgust and said, "Is this all you got?" I could see myself being thrown from the cab by the way he was looking at me.

I said, "I got two rolls of film you can have." He quickly took my money and my film. As we speedily traveled across the Oakland Bay Bridge, I kept telling him about my love predicament and how it blinded me from the reality of the need for money. We continued to drive and as we got closer to my destination, he looked at me shaking his head in disbelief and to my surprise he handed me the film and my money as if to

Linda in India in 1984

say, "a person with a story like that is either lying or in love." He did not look too happy about giving my money back. It has to be a miracle when a cab driver does not charge you a fare!

Here, I was again safe aboard ship at my post with a smile on my face knowing that I was in love.

During my time overseas, Linda and I corresponded by mail. I would get the sweet smelling letters with a stick of gum. The call for

Linda Parent and sisters; Lensie Brewster and Hattie Brewster with Linda, Frances and Tonya

mail came over the intercom, "Mail Call." This was a time of suspense when the men would gather around waiting for their name to be called to receive a most prized possession -- a letter from home. However, sometimes the letters would contain words that were as venomous as snake bites telling them of a death in the family or "it's over". That dreadful "Dear John" letter sometimes came to an unsuspecting sailor, and often resulted in breaking the very will of that sailor. Mail call was a time of tears and laughter. I have seen the Navy's finest break down and cry after reading the contents of a "Dear John" letter. I got a Dear John letter every time I was privileged to receive any mail from Stateside. Of course, *it* is my name, "Dear John."

After, receiving letters from Linda for months, I decided to reply with a proposal to ask her hand in marriage. I anticipated an unequivocal, "Yes." Weeks seemed like months before I got a response from Linda. When the letter finally

John and Linda at youngest daughter's Wedding

arrived, I hurried to open it, with hope to see in bold letters "Yes!" But the words I read were a question: "Are you sure?" I did not know how to take, "Are you sure?" I was upset with the question.

"How dare you ask me..."ARE YOU SURE?" After all I had done: traveling for miles to see you and all those "Romeo and Juliet" quotes and now you ask me, "Are you sure?" After reading more of the letter, I realized that Linda was not asking this question to insult me; it was because she wanted to be reassured of my love for her. She wanted me to be sure, so that she could be sure. She said that we should pray more about it. She gave a timeline of three months for examination.

It was frightening to me, because it raised doubt in my mind. I did not know if I was sure. Yes, I loved her, but was I ready to make this life long commitment of marriage. Now, I knew I had to ask

84

John and Linda dating 1969

myself some hard questions. Will I love her after life takes its toll on her? You know, weight gain, loss of hair and all that comes with time. Was my motive really only for physical satisfaction? Thank God for allowing me to look beyond the physical attraction so that I could see the whole person, while we were away from each other. This was the best thing for us because it made us think more objectively. I became more serious in my reflections and deliberations.

After months, she said "Yes!" and I got more excited. I wanted to get back to the Pacific Northwest as quickly as possible. This was the woman I wanted to marry. I had made up my mind that I wanted to spend a lifetime with Linda.

We finally got married October 15, 1970 a year before my Navy service was over. The logic for the timing of our marriage was based upon what I called the "win" principle. After all, I had to go back to Vietnam for my final cruise. I had been blessed to return safely twice before, I did not know what the odds would be on a third cruise. Why not wait until I returned? I knew if I were killed, my wife would receive benefits; and if I lived, it would allow me to take the advantage of the benefits that were available for those that were married.

85

Married October 15, 1970

The Navy had priority on where I could go. I wanted so badly to go to Tacoma, Washington before my ship left Alameda, California for my final cruise. The Captain made it an order for no one to leave the Bay Area the two weeks before we were to leave. This put me in a dilemma, I wanted to get married before leaving, now what? Do I go "AWOL" or do I be a good sailor and, "suck it up" and be miserable for the next nine months. Even though love had a powerful influence on me, I was not stupid. I remembered an old proverb, "If Mohammed can't go to the mountain then the mountain should come to Mohammed." This may not be the correct quote, but it fits my situation.

My orders forbid me from going to Tacoma and I knew it would be a complicated task to get Linda to come to Alameda, California. You may ask, "What was so difficult about Linda coming to California to get married?" I called Linda to let her know that I could not come and I needed her to come to me. Linda was only seventeen and had recently graduated from High School. She was still staying at home. Her parents and her Pastor were very concerned about her traveling to meet a sailor to get married. The neighbors and the church members would have a field day with the rumors, "I knew she was not all that good! Look she had to get married out of town and to a sailor. She must have gotten into trouble." Those rumors would have been unfounded because Linda was unwavering in her determination that there would be no intimacy before marriage. This perhaps was the main objection against her coming to me in California: her parents and the Pastor wanted to save Linda's good name. I did not care about saving a good name. I wanted to save a *good thing*. The Bible did say in Proverbs 18:22, "*Whoso* finds a wife finds a *good thing,* and obtains favor of the LORD." I had the Lord's favor; however, I needed the favor of her parents and Bishop T. L. Westbrook

John and Linda dressed EWU gear

Their objection to Linda coming to me did not settle very well with me; I just knew I was in love and ready to get married. Selfish as it may have seemed to her parents, I did not care how they felt about preserving the dignity of their daughter's name.

I was not thinking from a parent's perspective. My reasoning had been distorted by the spell of *LOVE*. It took many intense phone calls to convince her parents I was serious and that I would

Linda and John going out

take care of their daughter. I finally got a yes from Linda's parents.

I sent her airline tickets and made plans to pick her up when her flight arrived. I went to the airport with joy expecting to see my future bride come down the corridor from the scheduled flight. I saw people coming off the plane, but no Linda! I knew she had to be on the plane. Maybe she was hiding and trying to surprise me? She had to be somewhere, was my thought. I waited until it was apparent that she was not on the plane. My mind thought of every negative thing: maybe she got sick; she changed her mind about marriage. I could not believe the love of my life was not on the plane. I left the airport greatly disappointed.

"How could she do this to me?" I asked Elder Starks, a friend who took me into his home in Oakland, California while my ship was docked in Alameda. I was so upset, I kept pacing the floor ranting, "How could she do this to me?" not thinking, maybe she was hurt or that maybe something happened over which she had no control. Elder Starks encouraged me to call to find out the problem.

I called and spoke with Linda and with sadness she told me that her Pastor, Bishop T. L. Westbrook was not giving his blessing for her to

88

come to California. When I heard this, I knew I needed to talk with the person that was hindering me from being with the girl I loved. I had never met Bishop Westbrook and at this time I only knew him as a problem.

I called Bishop with my prepared speech, he answered with a calm, but firm bass voice, "Hello." I could not say a word, I was frightened and I lost my train of thought.

He repeated, "Hello." I mustered enough courage to identify who I was.

He said, "Son, I know what you want to do, but I do not think it would be good for a daughter of the church to be going away to marry." Before he could complete his statement, I said with disappointment that I did not think it was right for him to stop Linda from coming to California. It did not take me long to realize that I was talking with a man of great principles. After talking with Bishop and listening to his reason, I let him know I understood what he was trying to do. He listened to me with reservations, but with empathy he consented to let Linda come to California. Linda finally arrived in Oakland, California and we were married October 15, 1970.

I had only two weeks to enjoy my wife. I was scheduled to leave for my final tour to Vietnam. The Lord knew I did not want to go overseas again. I had been overseas several times before, and I thought the Navy was requiring too much of me to ask me to go once again. I tried everything I knew to get my order changed, putting in a request to have my order changed; but with no avail. I was told my only recourse was to have someone trade with me from another ship. I had experience with a miracle trade before, why not again? The trade must come from someone on another carrier that was coming from a West Pac Cruise. In other words, the person would exchange stateside duty for sea duty. This was not likely to happen, because sea duty was not as desirable as state side duty. However, I had to try it. I made contact with someone on the USS Constellation another aircraft carrier which was just returning from West Pac (Western Pacific Cruise). However, after many weeks of dialogue the person declined. I resolved in my heart that I would be going overseas again.

After two weeks of marriage, I was shipped out to sea. I would not see my wife for nine months. It was hard for me, but I had memories of the girl I loved. I knew if I held out, I would be out of the navy when I returned.

While away I kept myself involved in ministry, which occupied my mind and kept me from getting too lonely, Yes, I missed my wife, but I had to do what I had to do.

The Nine months away passed slowly because I counted each day awaiting the return to my wife and the start of a new career. Through many nights and days of prayer, the ship made it back to Alameda shipyard in California. I could not wait to catch a flight to the Pacific Northwest to see the girl I had left nine months before. With enough money to catch a taxi, I left the ship that had been my home for three years, three months and twenty-seven days.

Looking over my shoulder I looked at that ship for the last time. I looked back with a smile of gratitude and walked forward to a life of equal challenges. However, this time I would share it with my wife. Immediately, I went to the airport to catch my flight to the Pacific Northwest. When I saw Linda in the distance waiting for me my heart beat rapidly. This beautiful, shy girl, whom I left nine months before, was now Mrs. Linda Penton, the woman of my life.

Group photo of the Forensic Unit of the Tacoma Police Department

25 years later at retirement with my son on the left

92

Chapter Eleven

THE REAL WORLD

The "love thing" soon turned into the reality of survival. The excitement of love can only keep you distracted for a little while until your stomach starts growling and you finally realize you are upstairs in your mother-in-law's house. When I had to look for a job, the smile on my face turned into a determined look. My wife let me know it "takes money, Honey."

One of my first jobs was a door-to-door salesperson, selling encyclopedias. I went door to door, but I could never convince anyone to buy. I knew I had to get a job that would at least pay me something for my effort, because it was not good to see the only food in volume "F" of an encyclopedia. I kept going to the employment office and they would give me various leads and some jobs were for only a short time. One such job was a toy salesman at the Sears downtown Tacoma to work in the Toys' Department. Selling toys to kids was not hard; it was collecting the money from the parents that was far more difficult. It was a seasonal job during the Christmas.

I made enough money to move from my mother-in-law's home into a one bedroom duplex in an old part of Tacoma called, "Lincoln Heights". It wasn't the best of places, but it was our place. We did not care that the floor was tilted in the bath room, which made it hard to keep the water from spilling from the bathtub. I couldn't complaint too much because I was only paying 69 dollars a month for rent.

I kept my name in the pool at the employment office and my frequent visits to the office helped the people get to know me better as I became very familiar with the workers there. Although I accepted every job that was given to me, I was looking for a job in photography. One evening about 9 PM, I received a call from one of the people from the employment office. I thought it was unusual to receive a call at that time because the office was closed. The person sounded as if she was giving me some secret information that would save the world. She said that the Police Department was taking applications for a photographer's job that had been newly created. I did not understand why I didn't see this job listed when I was at the employment office. Well, it did not matter, I was getting privileged information. I went the next day to be interviewed at the Police Department. I was the last in line. When the interviewer got to me, I was feeling a little self conscious and he appeared to be cynical when he asked me to go to the lab and process and develop several photos. I knew he did not expect me to know how to do it. The photo lab was like putting a fox into a chicken coop, I was on familiar grounds because this was what I had done in the navy for several years. The tasks were simple, I was asked to process and print a series of photos. I completed the assignment so quickly, I had a debate whether I should delay coming out of the lab. I wanted to avoid the impression of arrogance. After they inspected my work, they were very surprised and impressed with the ability I had, and I was hired without any farther interviews. I didn't know at the time that I would be the first professional photographer ever hired by the Tacoma Police Department

I was thrust into a subculture that was in some ways the same as the Navy. The same type of ranking order as the military, but their missions were different. The Navy was to protect the nation from the enemy outside the country and the police were to protect the citizens from the enemy within the country. The problem, sometimes, was trying to keep a positive mind and keep from becoming paranoid because of the day-to-day crisis I had to deal with in the world of fighting crime.

I was not sure I could handle the crime scenes that were described to me by those who were not in favor of my being in the department. They gave graphic descriptions of the blood and the gore at homicide scenes; as if this would discourage me from pursuing my newly found job. I thought, "Maybe this is not a blessing after all." My desire to be a photographer was based more upon the fact that I wanted to capture the beauty of life not the horror of life.

I regained my focus after I weighed the alternative: *FOOD* or *NO FOOD*. It's funny how that drives a man. The darkroom was my haven for consultation with God. The darkroom was my prayer closet. I hoped that I would never see the horrors that were described to me. However, I knew that was part of the job. At the beginning, the photographer's job was not permanent; the job was for nine months. It was an experiment by the Police Department to see if it would relieve the patrol officers from the photographic responsibility so that they could focus more on police work. The impact of my service as a photographer was positive and increasingly the department would become more dependant upon me. Over time my position would become essential.

During this probationary period I did not have to go out on serious crime scenes such as homicides. But I did have to process the film and print the pictures from each scene. Just the photos, alone, were enough to turn your stomach. Through God's grace I developed a tolerance to the photos. The Photo Lab was under the Identification Unit and my boss was head of the Identification Unit. The people that worked in the Identification Unit were well paid, because to be an Identification Officer the skill level was much broader. Special training and educational requirements were necessary to be an Identification Officer. Photography was just one of those required skills.

Finger print identification, crime investigation and evidence processing were some other skills that were required. I knew that if I was going to seek permanent employment with the Police Department it would be as an Identification officer.

While working as a photographer, I would learn from the Identification Officers the various techniques and I would read the reference books. My hope was that, by the time my tenure was up, maybe an opening for Identification Officer would become available. I knew by the way the others in the Identification Unit were acting around me, they thought this was not even a possibility. In fact, when one of the supervisors heard that I was trying to learn more and planning to apply for the job, some day; he looked at me with disdain and said, "I know what you're thinking about doing, but don't even try it because you will not pass the test anyway." He did not know his words were more encouraging when they were meant to be discouraging. This sounded like a replay from the Navy. I was quite familiar with this type of challenge.

I discovered that there would be a test given in several months, because one of the Identification Officers was expected to retire sometime the next year. I became more determined to learn about the various duties that were required. I took the books home to read. The closer the time came for the test to be given, I became more uncertain whether I should take it or not, after all this would take me to those horrible, gross crime scenes.

97

I could not let anything or anyone discourage me from seeking a permanent job, even if the job would be difficult. I knew I could do well. The job training as a photographer exposed me to the technical functions of Identification Officer.

If an opening became available they required a civil service test. The test was given before my temporary position as photographer ended. This was great! I had gained valuable knowledge that helped me to pass the test and become the first Africa American Identification Officer. My struggles were not over after passing the test; I had to continue to prove myself to the others. I knew that there were many that thought Blacks were not as intelligent as the Whites. Sometimes I made a mess of things when I tried to prove that I was as good as the next person. I found that it was better not to take yourself too seriously, but you must be serious about life. You must laugh at your mistakes before others laugh and if you are corrected, do not take it personally. I was so eager to prove myself on a burglary scene I ended up solving my own crime.

Chapter Twelve

SOLVING YOUR OWN CRIME

I had been with the Tacoma Police Department for several years before I was given assignment in the field. I was finally called to the office by the supervisor of the Identification section and given an assignment to process a business burglary. I was excited because this would give me a chance to show my "Sherlock Holmes" skills. After all, how can a rookie mess up a burglary scene?

John doing Lab Photography

When I arrived at the scene I met with the contact person from the business. I was instructed by the victim that the scene was the company truck parked at the home of one of the drivers. I immediately tried to put myself in the mind of the unknown suspected burglar. This was one of my first crime scenes. This was my chance to impress the skeptics about my qualifications

When the driver showed me the truck, the lock on the truck was unlocked, I said to the victim with certainty, "I can see that the suspect has a key because I don't see forced entry." I opened the door of the truck trailer very slowly, being careful not to distribute any possible evidence. After opening the door, I discovered the contents of the trailer: boxes of packaged cookies were scattered on the floor. I said silently, "It had to be kids."

There were a large number of boxes containing one dozen packages of cookies per box. It was strange, I noticed the boxes were not opened, yet they were scattered in the trailer, as if someone had ransacked the trailer.

I was giving the victim my "play-by-play" Sherlock Holmes theory of how the burglar went about his deed of doing the crime. I used technical terms to impress the victim, I would say, "This was the suspect's modo (Mode of operation). The victim was all ears, he was fascinated by my knowledge or by the words I was using. He did not know I was just repeating what I had heard on the TV Police dramas. As we went through the scene the victim insisted that it was possible that a large quantity of cookies were taken by the burglar. After looking around I did not see any trace evidence, not even a fingerprint was left.

I said to the victim, "In order for me to be more thorough I must take the boxes that appear to be handled by the suspect into the lab to be processed."

The boxes containing the cookies were large. I told the victim with confidence I was sure I would get fingerprints from the boxes since they looked to have been handled by the suspect. I told him to carefully remove the cookies and I would take the empty boxes. He insisted that I take the boxes with the cookies. I guess it did not matter to him since they were considered damaged goods.

I took the boxes containing twenty four dozen cookies. My dilemma was how I was going to dispose of the cookies after removing them from the boxes. I had to get rid of the cookies before I could process the boxes. I decided to give the cookies to the Officers. They thanked me and congratulated me for a job well done. I was a regular "Good Ole Boy", I had just shared the spoils with the gang and now I was being accepted as one of   them.

We were eating cookies with our coffee and talking about how my good work would certainly lead to the arrest of this infamous cookie burglary. Then I got a call, it was the victim, I knew he was calling to give me more information that would lead to the arrest of my suspect. His voice was excited, as I enjoyed the cookies while wiping the crumbs from my mouth. Then he said to me, "I did an inventory of the stock after you left and I have talked with the driver, he found that the only inventory missing were the boxes of cookies you took as evidence; and by the way, the boxes were scattered when the diver made a sudden stop when he parked the truck. In other words, there was no burglary."

I was shocked and embarrassed as I looked around the office, cookie crumbs everywhere and the officers were still thanking me for their lunch. I did not have the courage to tell the cookie eating officers that I was the Burglar. I was so happy that "the victim" did not want the cookies back. When it became known to the other officers that they had eaten cookie from a non-crime, I was known as the "Cookie Caper."

Being an apprentice in the department had its challenges. I learned that it is better to just state the facts and not to assume anything. The attitude of an optimist helped me realize that I was just in a training period and it was expected that I would make mistakes. However, I knew my mistakes were being considered "just cause" for me to be terminated before I could take the examination for permanent employment as an Identification Technician.

Chapter thirteen

MOVING ON UP

I spent many hours in the Photo Lab consulting God about my future with the Police Department. My wife was pregnant with our first daughter during the time of my apprenticeship. I knew I needed a permanent job to support my family. While praying God gave me the assurance that He would give me the strength I needed to handle anything I would encounter at the police department.

Testing time finally came; I was as ready as I could have been. I took the test knowing that I was blessed to have been working around the Identification Officers. I had gained a considerable knowledge about the duties of the Identification Officers, which was very helpful to me. It gave me an edge on the test. To my surprise the test results showed that I passed and now I had to wait until a position became open. During the time of waiting, I had the security of my job as a photographer.

I knew my stay in the leaning apartment would be a thing of the past when my job became permanent. We stayed in the duplex for several months. The landlord found out about my pending upgrade on my job and told us that the rent would be going up as soon as by salary went up. He was really putting us on notice that we had to move. It was a strange feeling being put out because you were making too much. I was always under the impression that you get put out for not making enough money. What a feeling!

I was really moving on up to the East side. You may remember the theme song from the old TV show about the Jefferson's, "Moving On Up." This was the first time I felt "class-ism" being imposed on me. Since I had to move, let me move in style, we made a decision to buy a new home. This was our first home. We found this new home on the corner on East 62nd and K Street for $18,500.00. The mortgage payment was $169.00 per month, just one hundred dollars more than what we were paying for the "leaning bath tub duplex."

We felt safe enough to start our family. Our first child, Veronica, was conceived during the time our country was going though the gas shortage. Service stations were rationing gas. They were open during daylight hours. Long lines were becoming a normal sight. People were getting to accept the long line. However, it was a problem when I began working grave yard shift; this was during my wife's final days of pregnancy. I did not get gas before going to work.

I told my wife, "Just don't have the baby tonight." My suggestion was not followed. It was the night Veronica decided to make her entrance into the world. While I was processing a burglary scene, I got a call on my police radio, I knew this was *it.* I quickly returned to the police station to get my car. When I got in the car it was very obvious that the gas needle was on empty. I knew I had to go to the east side and bring my wife to the hospital which was on the south end. I almost panicked, but I knew I could make it if I did not take any detours.

When I arrived at home, my wife was blowing and pushing. I was more nervous than she was. "Hang in there," I said with the added uncertainty of whether I was going to make it to the hospital on an empty tank. Every moment counted. The baby was on *his* way! I was concentrating so much on gas level, I got lost, I passed the street where the hospital was and found my self in a maze in Old Town Tacoma. In the darkness of night I kept driving and praying. Out of the darkness, I saw at a distance the lights from the emergency sign of Tacoma General Hospital.

We made it just in time, very shortly after our arrival the doctor came to me, "Mr. Penton, your wife and your daughter are all right."

I said, "Daughter!!??" I knew I had asked God for a son. I had told everybody at work and church that I was going to have a son. I guess you can ask for what you want, but you must accept what you get. My disappointment quickly changed to exhilarating joy, when I saw this beautiful child that my wife and I made possible.

We have three children Veronica Penton (Dawkins), John Wayne Penton, Jr.; and Marzette Penton (Mondin).

I became a father on a mission. I wanted to be there for my children as they grew up. Working with the Police Department made it difficult to be with them at times because of the various shifts I had to work. My wife accused me of not always being there in the night when the children were babies. We had some turbulent times in the early part of our marriage. However, God helped Linda and me to keep working at our relationship. It pays to keep working through your problems. I can only say, "Thank God for forgiveness!" We must be strong for each other. My wife sacrificed many things to be available for me and the children.

The kids helped us keep focus on what was important in our family. Even with my working schedule our children had both of us around them to encourage them. My wife and I knew early on, that Veronica, Wayne and Marzette were champions.

Chapter Fourteen

THE RAISING OF THREE CHAMPIONS

When our children became old enough to understand the importance of making right choices, I knew it was time for me to make the time to talk with them and instill within them the kind of values to shape their minds; that lead to successful lives. I knew that education was the key that would open the door to get them to where I desired them to be. My intent was that they view college as an extension of high school. And of course, there wouldn't be a break in between. Again, my concern was that they would take a break and get caught up in buying things they couldn't afford and would have to work at McDonalds just to pay for some toy (car) they wanted. Too often parents buy their graduates a car and give them a key in hopes that their children will learn responsibility through making payments and maintaining the vehicle. This is a very noble thought, but when you think about it, this causes them to make the car a priority. In the end it consumes their time and college really becomes secondary.

The family in early years

As you know, a college education is a major investment for most households. I realized that I had two choices: I could put money away which would take a whole lot longer since my three champions were very close in age, or I could help them obtain scholarships. The latter was more feasible. Our children knew that they were going to get scholarships before they knew what the word meant. When each child was in elementary school, we began shaping their mind for college.

Veronica at 4 years old

Yes. We constantly encouraged our champions to excel in their studies. Academic scholarships were far more competitive, but I figured better grades would give them an edge when contending for athletic scholarships. I knew that if they were forced to be involved with sports against their will, it was not going to last. So I had to discover what each of them enjoyed doing. Through enrollment in various sports, they each learned which sport they could do naturally: softball, basketball and track. Although they played each of these sports fairly well, I noticed how swift that could move up and down the court. It was a cinch. Track and field would be their winning ticket.

How do you keep a child interested from elementary through high school? My wife and I realized early on that we had to take a very active role in their lives. Whenever they participated in an event, we were there to cheer them with positive feedback on their performances. At times it was obvious that they lacked self-confidence; we had to constantly reassure them that it was all right and that there would always be another chance to do better. While giving up because they didn't do well wasn't an option, I often told them, "You are not going to quit, because you did not come out first or

109

Wayne at 4 years old

because your team lost. However, you can choose to change the sport if you no longer have an interest." I taught them that being involved with sports was like having a part time job that would eventually pay large dividends; namely a scholarship.

I recall one of those days... all the kids were tired and wanted to go to work like their friends who were working at McDonalds. It was time to reason with them. I asked, "How much does McDonald pay per hour?"

One of them replied with uncertainty, "$2.75 an hour."

I then asked. "How long will it take to earn $100,000? That's what it would cost for four years in the best college." They knew immediately it would take a lot longer than they wanted to endure. This logic must have worked, because they continued with track and field.

As time progressed, I looked for new ways to help them develop and build endurance and speed. The game of catch was used as a timing discipline. To start, I lined all three kids against the outside wall of the house. The rule of our catch game was that each of them had to catch the ball ten-consecutive times before they would be allowed to quit. If one missed, we started all over again.

Marzett at 4 years old

Together we counted, "one, two, and three…" getting to the higher numbers I threw harder. I saw the tension in their faces as the numbers grew. It was usually when we got to number ten that one of them dropped the ball. This really motivated them to support one another, encouraging each other to do better. It also promoted wholesome competition.

My son did not want to be outdone by his older sister. Veronica could always beat Wayne running during elementary school. She was also a better basketball player in those early years too. As time went on, Wayne became stronger and naturally out ran Veronica. However, as they competed against other kids in their age group, they demonstrated that they could run and play with the best of them.

During the summer we enrolled them in the Junior Olympics Program. This was a great opportunity for them to compete with children from other areas. Veronica, Wayne, and Marzette did so well in their local competitions that they were afforded the opportunity to compete with kids across the United States. I knew that the Junior Olympics would get place them in clear view of numerous college coaches. This was the scouting ground for college coaches. I had heard that even

111

the NCAA rules prohibited the coaches from talking directly to kids before their senior year in high school, but it was not any rule I knew that prohibited the parent from talking to the coach. While the kids were on the field preparing for the various events, I was scouting for college coaches. Sometimes they were easy to spot. At other times, I used my investigative police skills. Once spotted, I strategically positioned my self next to them; throwing hints about what kids to watch. I tried to do this without telling them who I was, but the pride I had for my kids would not let me conceal this fact. I was screaming to the top of my lungs calling their names embarrassing my kids. Yet, I knew they were as proud of their mother and me as we were proud of them.

Our children were not always first place contestants. They often put themselves down when they weren't first, but we constantly reminded them that doing their best would always make them winners. We instilled in them that the same is true in life. We never got down on them for not coming in first. We rewarded them just for showing up and doing their best. I knew there had to be balance in their lives, so we made sure that they had plenty of time to play and spend time with their friends. However, they did not lose sight of the bigger picture. SCHOLARSHIPS!

By the time the kids got to high school, the Pentons had earned a reputation as track and field celebrities drawing attention from the local newspaper. At least one of our kids was featured almost every track season for several years. When we moved from the north end of Tacoma to Lakewood, the headlines in the sport section of the paper read, "The Pentons Moved: A Gain for Lakewood." I was happy about all the publicity, but a little embarrassed at times, especially, when I heard some of the not so favorable comments coming from parents who were as passionate about their kids as we were. You know how it is when you're the one at the top... you're the one that everybody has to beat.

Even with all the popularity, local colleges did not express the kind of interest we anticipated. During the summer of Veronica's senior year, the family took a tour around the United States in a motor home, with the sole purpose of introducing our children to colleges across the nation. We knew that we had reared three champions, but it was time to make them known to those in position to extend scholarships. My marketing strategy was to expose them to colleges with good track programs: Michigan State, Howard University, and Louisiana State University were all excited and impressed with the interest and time we had invested, yet we sensed that we would get a "maybe" at the most, if they would seriously consider them at all. I consoled myself with the fact that it was more than we had before the tour.

Returning home after a grueling 9,000-mile, two-week trip, I immediately called several of the colleges and universities within Washington State and implied that several of the universities around the country were interested in my champions. And believe it or not, shortly thereafter the letters and telephone calls came. Since Veronica was a high school senior, legally she was the only one who

Veronica High School

A straight arrow who hopes she's on target

Penton sets lofty goals in track — and in life

By Doug Drowley
For The News Tribune

Veronica Penton is a junior with a mission. Last season, as a sophomore at Lincoln High School, Penton finished fifth in the girls Class AAA 100 hurdles at Mad Track VII. She then added an eighth in the 300s.

This year Penton set her sights higher.

"I'm looking for second or first," she said of the state meet. "If I take second — and PR (set a personal record) — then I'll be satisfied. I'd like to run in the 44s (300). I am really running for time, even though I wouldn't mind winning. I've taken off at least two seconds from last year."

Penton whipped the field at the Narrows League

> **I'm known as a straight person, and I'm respected for it.**

sub-district meet two weeks ago where she ran a 45.2 300 hurdles and a 14.8 (her PR) in the 100.

But Penton's best efforts might not even be on the track.

Through her leadership class at Lincoln, Penton will be involved with planning and carrying out a workshop dealing with drinking and driving. It is a subject she said she feels strongly about.

"I feel strongly about everything, especially drinking and drugs," she said. "I got that from my dad. I state my opinions about things, but it is more as an example. People around me, my friends, know I don't go to parties and drink. I'm known as a straight person, and I'm respected for it."

Penton said she doesn't have the answers about

keep being an example. I can be a person who doesn't have to try that. People think I can be a wimp (because of that). Yet everyone knows where I stand. They just think I'm kind of boring."

Boring or not, Penton has had her sights set on spring on Star Track — and also on Karen Word-toson, the Kent-Meridian star who head Veronica in the Sammamish Invitational.

To get where she is, Penton has had to work. Her coach, Gil Boyd, said she is always willing to do whatever it takes.

"She is remarkable young lady," Boyd said. "Her performance in class is just as good or better than on the track. She is a hard worker. Veronica is always one of the last ones to leave the track each day. She works at her event hard — goes at it diligently."

Penton has been running the hurdles for several years now. She said she first became interested back in the seventh grade.

"In the seventh grade, I saw older girls looking at them," Penton said. "I was the type of girl that wanted to try to do something new, especially when I found them interesting."

So, during the eighth grade, Penton took up the 200 hurdles.

"Coaches kept telling me I had natural talent," she said. "I lost only by two-tenths and ran a 15.7 in the eighth grade. Even though I took second, I knew it was my race. I did take (ntry) in the ninth grade and broke the record. It was 15.2, and I ran a 15.8. I knew it was mine. I was up there with high-school age."

The 300s were a different story. In fact, Penton fell into them more by accident than anything.

"It was just a love affair she had, per se, with the 100 hurdles," Boyd said. "In a meet against Steilacoom last year, she got a chance to participate in the 300s."

"Coach put me in at the last minute because we needed those extra points," Penton said. "I was kind of excited at first because I had never run anything longer than the 200. To be honest, I didn't like them at first; they took all my energy from me because I hadn't built a tolerance for it."

The longer distance became easier as the year went along, however. Boyd said the 300s might even be her

could be contacted. Washington State University (WSU), University of Washington (UW), and Eastern Washington University (EWU) sent invitations to view their campuses. Things were looking up!

Like a professional athletic agent seeking to negotiate the best contract, I saw the light at the end of the tunnel. Although I did most of the talking

114

with the coaches, my wife did most of the encouraging. It was

difficult for our children to maintain normalcy with all the stress that was caused by the

❖ BIG SKY CONFERENCE/
SEAFIRST BANK
TRACK & FIELD
CHAMPIONSHIPS

May 19-22, 1993
Spokane, Washington

Defending Big Sky Conference
400 Meter Hurdles Champion
Veronica Penton of EWU.

GILL EASTERN GILL

Veronica College years

attention and the demand to excel. I'm sure the kids would not have made it with me alone. My wife was the balance that kept the kids from giving up. At times my motives were selfish. I just wanted them to get a scholarship so that I wouldn't have to pay for their college education. Selfish as it may have been, I knew it would benefit them. I also knew that keeping my children involved in sports and focused on maintaining good grades, would keep them from being drawn into the "gang" culture that was very prevalent during their junior and high school years. It was not easy for the kids because I was paranoid. I worked with the police department and was aware of the criminal mind. My children

115

got tired of me coming home warning them about some of the kids at school. Of course, they did not believe a word I said, or at least they did not indicate that they were taking me seriously. During their adolescence, children tend to think that their parent's advice is more destructive than the gang culture.

It was hard for me not to be influenced by the things I saw at work. I tried to mix my paranoia with humorous reflections, to foster a lighter approach on the day's occurrences. I noticed earlier in their childhood, that our children loved to hear about my childhood. They constantly asked me to repeat some of the stories to their friends. I was a great storyteller according to my children. Therefore, I would somehow mix conventional wisdom with my stories. It was like putting sugar with bitter medicine to make it more palatable. It must have worked, because they turned out okay. I must admit that I was not a perfect father. I thank God for His mercy! It was very difficult for me to admit my vulnerability to my children, but I am glad we had discussions that brought out some of those issues. For instance, when I dealt with people in public, I was this smiling lovable person, but the family knew another side of me that was not so pleasant.

I did not trust the kids and I let them know it. I told them that I did not trust them, because I didn't trust myself. I was trying to justify my negative actions. I found out later after the kids grew up, my distrust of them had a negative impact

116

on them. However, the good carried more weight than the bad. Thanks be to God.

Through the good and the bad, we declared that there were three champions among us: Veronica, Wayne, and Marzette. They proved it many times. During a district track competition in Veronica's senior year, she was favored and won the three hundred meters hurdle. In that event, the contenders had to come out in first and second place to qualify for competition in the State. It was very important and the community sensed it. This was an event in which all the schools across the county participated. The newspaper reporters were there; as were my wife and I in nervous anticipation. We didn't take anything for granted, because we had become veterans of track and fields upsets. We watched the various events and shared with other parents as they were shouting in the audience, encouraging their kids into the champion circle.

Let me digress. This event was considered the premier of all events; the women's three hundred meters hurdle. Within the crowd we heard comments about whom they expected to win. It did not matter what their expectations were, my wife and I knew that in less than 15 seconds we would all know.

The starter raised the gun and shouted, "Get set." Bang the gun went off! The crowd roared with shouts from the crowd, each parent shouting their child's name, some were shouting the name of the school, cheering, "Go, go, go."

My wife and I lost all dignity as we screamed to the top of our voices, "Come on Veronica, you can do it." Above all the shouts, I heard this beautiful high-pitched shout coming from my usually quiet, mild-mannered wife, "Go Veronica, go Veronica, you can make it."

The girls in all eight lanes started off well. That is until Veronica took the lead. The crowd roared louder as the distance between Veronica and the others lengthened. Then, suddenly, Veronica clipped a hurdle around the second turn and fell to the ground. The noise turned into a frightening awe of disbelief. On some of the faces of the parents was a sign of relief, because their kids finally had a chance to win; after all, the champion was lying motionless on the ground.

At that point, things slowed in motion. The other runners continued passing Veronica. I didn't know how badly she was hurt, but it seemed like she was down on the ground for several minutes. I started to run over to see what was going on. Suddenly she moved and then got up! The crowd turned their attention away from the girls who were leading the pack and started cheering for our determined champion. I could not believe it. Veronica resumed her place on the track. She kept running until she caught up and kept running until she reached the finish line where she collapsed.

Her knee was scraped and she was exhausted. The media gathered around with their cameras and notepads. The headline in the sport section read, "Penton Survives Fall." She had done the impossible. After falling and losing the lead, she regained her composure and completed the race, qualifying for competition in the State. Veronica took first place in the Washington State High School Three Hundred Hurdle Competition.

Veronica accepted a full scholarship to Eastern Washington University. She continued to succeed in Track and Field until she graduated. Today, she is a high school teacher, married, and the mother of two sons.

My son Wayne, our second champion, is shy and funny. He became known as the brother of the fastest girl in track, but he wanted to be known for his own achievement. That was great motivation for the macho-ego. Wayne finally got his chance. Although known for his speed in track and field, he was always in the shadow of his sister, Veronica; that is, until I gave into the constant request of the coach who wanted Wayne to play football. My opinion was that he was not big enough. I thought you had to be big and mean to play football. Wayne did not fit that criterion. He was fast, so I thought track and field were going to be his ticket to college. The coach convinced me to let him try out for the team. Though reluctantly, I said, "Yes", I felt I might as well let him get this out of his system. Furthermore, I knew that after he was hit a couple of times, he would retreat to the track. To my surprise he endured the hitting throughout the practices and made the team. Even after he made the team, I thought it was just a matter of time.

Maybe after the first real game, when the hitting was harder, he would be back on track.

The first game clashed with my work schedule, so I was unable to attend. When I got home that night, I wanted to hear that Wayne had learned his lesson and that he had resolved that track was best for him. Instead, I saw a smiling face.

There were no bruises, or broken bones. There was no doubt that something had happened. Had he met a girl at the game?

Wayne High School Football

Bruce Kellman/The News Tribune

After racing for Lakes this weekend, Wayne Penton will turn his attention to Cal football.

Love of sports runs through family of champion sprinter

By Corey Brock
For The News Tribune

John Penton always envisioned his son as a baseball player.

Not a sprinter, surely not a football player — a baseball player.

After all, baseball was — and still is — Penton's first love. Coming from a small town in Louisiana, Penton used to toil on the baseball diamond under the hot sun for hours. He even had the opportunity to face Vida Blue in a high school state championship game.

"I remember two things about that game," Penton said. "We won the game, 1-0, and I didn't get a hit."

"I've always loved baseball."

Years later, Penton's son, Wayne, a senior at Lakes High School, still laughs when he hears that story.

"Playing baseball in that old hick town in Louisiana," the younger Penton said with

Logan said. "He's an outstanding athlete and student (3.0 grade-point average) who is always willing to help others.

"I was pretty happy when I found out he was coming to Lakes. I heard stories that he might be moving ... but I wasn't sure until I saw him prior to his junior season."

Penton attended Lincoln High School his freshman and sophomore years before moving into the Lakewood area in the fall of 1990. The move raised a few eyebrows.

"It was just a simple move," John Penton said. "We were getting ready to move anyway. It was just a matter of finding somewhere suitable for our family.

"It had nothing to do with getting out of the city or anything like that."

The move came after older sister Veronica graduated and moved on to Eastern Washington University, where she won the 400-meter hurdles at the Big Sky Championships on Saturday.

And Wayne and Veronica aren't the only Pentons active in track.

"My youngest daughter, Marzette, is something else," John Penton said. "It looks like she's turning

The News Papers kept reporting

121

HIGH S(

Bruce Kellman/The News Tribune
Lakes' Wayne Penton, left, edges Foss' Randy Townsend at the tape to win the 100 meters.

Penton streaks, Lakes routs field at Tacoma Invitational

By Doug Drowley
The News Tribune

Exhaustion was draped across the faces of Lakes' Wayne Penton and Foss' Randy Townsend.

They stood together. Each bent deeply at the waist, supporting himself with hands on knees. But both managed to smile as they chatted.

Penton had just pulled away from Townsend and fellow Lancer Shawn Moss to win the 400 meters in a state best 48.4 seconds.

TACOMA INVITATIONAL

state-best 48.2 seconds. The old mark of 42.5 was set by Lincoln in 1983.

Despite the three victories, it wasn't a perfect day for Penton. After winning the 400, he was forced to scratch out of the 200 with tightness in his groin.

"We didn't want to push him," Lakes' coach Warren Logan said. "Wayne had a good day. He ran a

"I wanted all three," Andrews said. "But my endurance (for the 400) is really down."

Bellarmine super-sophomore Sarna Renfro ran the 1,600 in a meet record — and state best — time of 4:58.7. Runner-up Kim Schmelka of South Kitsap (5:04.3) also ran quicker than the old mark of 5:06.3, set last spring by Bellarmine's Joline Stseheli. Renfro added a victory in the 800 in 2:18.6, another state best, and helped the Lions' 400 relay team to a third

The News Papers were a great help in keeping the Penton Name in the mind of the colleges

122

I just came out and asked him. "Well, how did you do tonight? He said with little emotion, "Dad I made five touchdowns."

"Five touchdowns!?!?" I queried with amazement.

Here he was: this 140-pound, shy boy had made five touchdowns in his first real game of football. I could not wait for the next game. I had to see my son play football. I knew he could catch a ball. He was well trained for that, but could he take a hit, that I wasn't sure about. When I saw him play, I was so impressed I forgot about college. My mind went straight to the NFL. And believe it or not, Wayne didn't have to worry about being hit too much, because he was so fast he would elude the defense most of the time.

I apologized to Wayne for doubting him. I was trying to protect him. The college recruiter used Wayne's first game to review him.

Wayne went on to become the Washington State Champion in the 400 meters, 2nd in the 100 and 200 meters. However, he received scholarship offers from most of the Pac 10 colleges for football. He finally settled for a full scholarship to the University of California at Berkeley. We had the pleasure seeing our son play against some the nation's great college teams. Unfortunately, in his third year of college, the medical staff discovered that Wayne had a congenital back problem that none of us knew about. They told him that it would not be good for him to continue playing football, because the chance of paralysis was a high risk.

Thinking about what could have happened early in his career only made me more grateful. Had this happened in high school, he wouldn't have had the opportunity to make his mark. The school decided to let him continue with his scholarship, even if he couldn't play football. It was at that point that Wayne decided to run track for the University of California until he graduated. Wayne is now married and is working on contract for Microsoft.

Marzette, our third champion, is our witty and girlish baby daughter. In contrast to Veronica who was more of a "tomboy", Marzette played with dolls. She had great interest in reading. Even more important, she was an honor student. Most of the time she had a book in hand curled up on the couch reading. I was not sure if Marzette would be an athlete. Her coordination skills weren't the greatest. However, she had the ability to jump. Once she was invited to participate in a sporting competition at Hershey, Pennsylvania. This was an annual event where youth from across the United States were selected for their athletic potential. Marzette had the potential, but I was not certain whether she would "turn it on." She didn't seem as excited about the event as we were. Her focus, like most kids, was where is the Hershey candy bar? But much to our surprise, we received a call from the east coast. It was Marzette. She was telling us how much fun she was having and how good the chocolate was. Of course I was anxious to know how she did in the competition.

SOUTH SPORTS

State's standout sprinter

Marzette Penton, center, wins the first heat of the 100-meter dash Friday at the West Central District AAA track meet in Federal Way. Penton recorded data near a top state times in the 100 and 200 the next day, making her the favorite at this weekend's Class AAA state championships at Lincoln Bowl in Tacoma.

Go Marzette!

Finally she said, "By the way I broke a record in the standing high jump."

"You did what?" I responded. I knew then that my "Mars" was destined to continue the Penton legacy. I continued to

encourage her to try other sports, because she was fast on her feet too, but her coordination skills tended to slow her down in some activities.

For a short time, she played basketball. The coach made good use of her jumping and rebounding abilities. She looked like a grasshopper; swiftly moving up and down the court. Marzette had an unusual way of running. She looked like she was sitting down in a chair with her legs and arms moving like the rods on a locomotive. She never seemed to be breathing hard. Needless to say, during track and field season I encouraged her to run. After all, she had a family tradition to uphold.

125

Marzette didn't have the competitive spirit that Veronica and Wayne possessed. She just ran and wherever she placed in the competition was okay. Her attitude was, "Well, O.K." I guess that was all right, because she won most of the time. I can't remember whether Marzette even sweated when she ran, but I do recall that her attitude began to change in her senior year. When the news that a new girl track star was on the horizon, Marzette's competitive drive kicked in. Mazette led in the 100 and 200 meters, as well as the long jump. Now, the word was out that there was another girl from another school district who was running faster than Marzette. That was good news for those who were tired of the Pentons dominating the tracks scene. They wanted to see a different champion, After all, Veronica and Wayne had been first place in their respective events during their senior years; it was fair to assume that Marzette would follow that trend. However, the competitors in her senior year were determined to defeat the last of the Pentons and she wasn't about to let that happen.

As my wife and I walked into the stadium, people gave us a less than genuine smile. They would say, "Good luck, Marzette" without even moving their lips.

I knew they weren't rooting for another Penton to win a State Championship. The premier race of the day was the 200 meters. That day I noticed a different look in Marzette eyes. She had the "eye of tigress" as my wife called it, whenever she saw this type of intensity in the kid's faces.

This was unusual for Marzette; this carefree little girl that loved to play with her dolls. But this day was special, one of girls had boasted about how she was going the beat Marzette. This gave Marzette the motivation I felt she needed. When the 200 meters started, Marzette ran as usual as though sitting down in her chair position. The other girls appeared to be putting forth more effort. Several of them pushed a step ahead. Marzette seemed to maintain the same pace until she felt challenged. Then she took the lead. We saw Marzette shift gears reaching down in her soul and turning on the after-burner. As she turned the final corner, it was hard to see who was in the lead. I was shouting, as I often did, "Go! Go! Go, Marzette." Just as the tape broke, Marzette landed at the finish line in first place.

What a way to keep the dream alive. I was asked by someone, "From which of you did the kids get their speed"? My answer is that it took both of us to make three Champions.

Marzette was offered several scholarships from Pac 10 Universities. Her choice was the University of Washington where she ran track. She graduated and is now married and working in Seattle, Washington.

Many doubted that our children would stay focused enough to become champions. And of course, our children are living proof that dreams can come true, but it does require perseverance. Some may say that they got a free ride through college. To them I say there are no free rides. They put many hours into training and preparing themselves. After all, time is money.

My wife and I are tremendously blessed with three champions. We see the same determination in them as they work at their various professions. They even come back home to visit with us. I noticed when the children call home they want to speak with their mother. I hear them talking as if they are taking with their best friend. This lets me know that the time spent in their development was one of the greatest investments we could have made.

John Penton, center, hugs daughter Marzette, while wife Linda and children Veronica and Wayne look on.

Thanks to Dad

Marketing pays off for athletic family

By Doug Brawley
The News Tribune

Veronica Penton gave her dad a Father's Day gift two days early. However it was just the latest in a long line of gift exchanges over the years between John Penton and his three children.

Veronica, the oldest offspring, graduated from Eastern Washington University on Friday.

For John, it was a festive day. All the hard work, the love and the six-year marketing program he set out for his freshmen came to fruition.

For Veronica, it was a rare opportunity to see her dad play just in his work as an event on which she was participating.

During her days at Truman Middle School and Lincoln High...

> "I don't think my role was very significant. I've just supported them in what they like to do and didn't let them quit if they were quitting just because it was hard."
> — John Penton

...were not just doing this for fun, although they are having fun. In fleness, John told his kids...

...potent combination.

But John and Linda Penton say they never made their kids participate in sports. Once the kids got involved in athletics, though, quitting was not going to be based on courses.

"I don't think my role was very significant," John said. "I've just supported them in what they like to do and didn't let them quit if they were quitting just because it was hard. If they quit because they really couldn't do it, fine."

Take Marzette and return. There was just so much there.

John figured the same would be true of Wayne and football.

"I wanted Wayne to play baseball, because I feel played baseball," John said. "I didn't have any idea he would play football...

This was a father day article in the Papers

Today's Champion Wayne,
Marzette and Veronica

129

Chapter Fifteen

ONE HOUR WITH BILL COSBY

Bill Cosby and John Wayne Penton, Sr. aren't two names you'd find on a billboard announcement as star and co- stars on Broadway, or some comedy show. Although some may recall my witty and light-hearted approach to life, Bill Cosby is definitely among the world's renowned comedians. But his name and mine together, is really more of a paradox. Even so, if I omitted my last name, Bill Cosby and John Wayne, would appear more natural.

As I mentioned earlier, Ebony magazine was my window to the world of prominent African-Americans. And of course, Bill Cosby was often featured there, an icon with whom I could identify.

Do you remember "I Spy" starring Bill Cosby? That was my favorite show, and one of the few programs depicting blacks in a positive light. This really gave me a sense of pride marking great significance during an era when black and white television was a big thing in my neighborhood. A more descriptive term could be "White" TV, as we seldom saw blacks on the screen.

It's funny how poverty breeds creativity. To add color, we taped blue cellophane paper to the television screen to see a black, blue Bill Cosby and white, blue Robert Culp. Wow...living color. Many years have past. Great feats and tragedies have been experienced by us both I'm sure; yet, it's both amazing and refreshing to see how Bill Cosby has kept his family a priority. He has maintained his dignity while achieving success in show business; further affirming that character is a person you are, rather than a role you play.

Because character and integrity were always high on my list of personal attributes, I continued to follow his career through the years. Finally, it was becoming more likely that my dream of meeting Mr. Cosby was within reach. Now, the face that I had enjoyed on the television screen was booking shows at the Washington State Fair. Yeah, live and in living color...so close yet still so far away. My work schedule at the Tacoma Police Department would not permit, but time and chance does come to us all.

Finally, Mr. Cosby was scheduled to perform at the University of Puget Sound (UPS) within close proximity of my home. I knew my chance had come. Not only did I want to see him, but to meet him. What were my chances? Suddenly, it was clear...I would invite him to my home for dinner. You can imagine what people thought when I told them. No one tried to stop me, because they knew it wasn't likely to happen. I didn't want to appear to be a star-crazed fan, because I was only one of many who desired the same privilege, so I had to be bold and courageous without being intimidating.

Bill Cosby and John. Above in his dressing room University of Puget Sound in the 80's and below at the Washington State Fair 2004

I went to UPS and found the people who were sponsoring the show and asked if it was okay to invite Bill Cosby to my home for dinner. They looked at me with in sarcastic disbelief and replied, "We don't know how to contact Bill Cosby directly, so we don't see how you are going to do it." I knew that they didn't think I was serious. One of them responded, "We don't care, go ahead."

My strategy was to send a letter with a picture of my family and menu of the proposed dinner.

First, I had to find a mailing address. Since Bill Cosby hosted the "Tonight Show" for Johnny Carson, this was a good place to start. I called the CBS television station; keeping in mind that to get the information required tact and discretion. To my surprise, someone picked up the phone, I inquired in my professional tone, "Is Bill doing the tonight show tonight"? I'm sure the guy thought I was someone important, because he allowed me to continue, " I know he is scheduled to do a show in Tacoma and I would like to extend an invitation to dinner." There was a slight pause, then the man asked "Is this for business"? I replied, "No"! Then he said, "don't tell anyone that I told you this, but you can contact his office at this number -------------
---." I dialed the number and got through. The person on the phone identified herself. I told her I needed an address to forward a dinner invitation to Bill Cosby. I guess she thought this was great. I didn't tell her much, as I felt that the letter, along with the pictures of my family would show that my

intent was pure. I mailed the letter that included a list of all the southern cuisine I thought he might enjoy and a picture of my family. After several weeks, to my surprise, I received a letter from Bill Cosby's Office. The letter thanked me for the invitation, but stated that due to his schedule he would not be able to attend.

Well, in my opinion I had reached second base. Now, I had an official letter with his secretary's name on it. This gave me some leverage. I now knew someone he knew. This would be useful. Since Mr. Cosby could not come to my house for dinner, I would meet him at the University.

I knew Mr. Cosby wore T-shirts with different emblems; like colleges and other organizations, so I decided to give him a T-shirt with our Church logo and name on it. What a promotion, I thought. Bill Cosby wearing a T-shirt that read, "Outreach Church of God In Christ"; the name of the Church I founded in Bremerton, Washington. We needed a little publicity, why not?

I remember the day of the show. I found out where Bill Cosby was going to be entering into the complex. Security was not an issue because of my employment with the police department. I waited in the hallway close to Mr. Cosby's dressing room. When he walked in the building, (away from the public), we made eye contact. I drew on my profession composure, as walked toward him. I greeted him saying, " Hi Bill", and then I asked, "Do you know F. -----S------"? He looked at me as

135

if puzzled. I knew he was thinking I must know this man, because he knows my secretary. He replied, in a sarcastic voice, "I ought to know her, she is my secretary."

By this time others were gathering around him introducing themselves as the progression continued toward his dressing room. I was within arm's reach. Arriving at the door of his dressing room, Mr. Cosby welcomed several people to join him. I was among them. There were several people behind me when he started to close the door. I explained, "Bill those are the people who are sponsoring the show", so he allowed then to enter.

There were five of us. With T-shirt in pocket, I waited for an opportunity to give it to him. It was finally my turn and my defining moment. I said, "I am the one who invited you to dinner." Mr. Cosby asked me where I lived. I told him not too far from where we were, but I went on to explain that I hadn't prepared dinner, because his secretary said he wouldn't have time. He sat down. I said jokingly, "Don't tell me that you never invited friends to dinner and ate it all before the guest arrived". Bill Cosby looked at me without a smile and said, "I am not going to tell you that, because it isn't worth telling."

Stunned by his remark, I asked myself. "Is he trying to be funny, or is he ranking on me?" Now, I was really uneasy about presenting my gift to him and thought it wise to be quiet. Fortunately, my humiliation was minimized, because no one else was aware of my plight.

136

Thirty minutes past. The pre-show activities could be heard in the background. A male singer had taken the stage and was sounding pretty good when Bill broke the silence and asked, "Does anyone know who's singing? Is he any good"? We looked at each with shrugged shoulders. That is until I retorted, "He must be good, because he is one of the people who came to see you Bill." He was dumfounded. He looked at me and pointed his finger saying, "You got me!"

For a second I thought he was upset. Then he grabbed my camera and asked someone to take our picture. My persistence was paying off, but I still hadn't given him my infamous gift.

Finally, it was curtain time for Bill, and of course, my last chance to complete my mission. As he passed me, walking toward the stage, the words slipped right out my mouth, "Bill I have a gift for you." He paused for a moment, and exclaimed, "Send it to me." I pulled the T- shirt from my pocket and handed it to him, being careful to conceal my logo.

The Crowd roared and erupted in applauds in anticipation of his presentation as Bill made his heroic entrance. He took my T-shirt that hanged from his back pocket and wiped the sweat from his face. I could only hope that he would realize that the most unassuming thing could be the most helpful.

Bill Cosby may not remember me. It would be nice if he did. Yet, he must know that his advocacy and promotion of education has been an inspiration. You might say that in a strange sort of way, he influenced and motivated me in my pursuit of a college education for my three children. With a degree of persistence and perseverance, all three of them earned their college degrees. But of equal importance, is the fact that my dream became a reality and so can yours. My encouragement is this: Ordinary people can impact extraordinary lives. Thanks Bill for the memory.

Bishop R. E. Altheimer. *I took this portrait in 1974. The Miracle is that the negative of this photo was lost during water damage in my home years later. It was discovered on the floor of my garage the year I was scheduled to go around the world. Ernett Altheimer was so generous and purchased his farther's portrait for $1400 to help me with my expense to travel around the world.*

Chapter Sixteen

AROUND THE WORLD IN 22 DAYS

Twenty two days makes this story a compelling "want to hear" adventure, but when the factual cost of *JUST* 200 dollars for airfare is mentioned, the need to know "how" becomes more compelling. No, I wasn't stuffed in a large box and stamped "Fed-Ex" and mailed to the other side of the world. It was the vacation of a lifetime.

A trip around the world is usually a dream realized only by the rich and famous...but what about the poor and the unemployed? At this time in life...I was unemployed and broke. I could not even take advantage of the "don't leave home without it" American Express card, because I did not have one. I did not have a credit card of any kind. However, a white guy—who attended my church, heard I had an opportunity to travel around the world; so he offered me his credit card and said that I could pay him back when I returned. His intention was noble, but can you imagine a black guy in some exotic place in the world paying

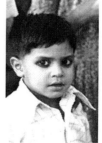

Boy of India

141

for his room with a white guy's credit card? I am sure someone else would have been writing this story if I had attempted to take my friend's offer. I did think about it.

Lady in the Market Place in Hong Kong

This adventure began at a time when I had quit my job at the Tacoma Police department after 10 years' employment to pursue my passionate call to full time ministry. The church I had organized several years before in Bremerton, Washington had grown to a little over 100 members. I felt that I needed to devote more time. Therefore I quit the department to have more time for ministry. I did not anticipate the transitory membership I had. I was counting on the membership to increase, but most of the supporters were military Navy families. Very shortly after I had committed my self to full time ministry, I learned the Navy had more influence and a large portion of the congregation got orders that moved them to other duty stations. I needed other income to supplement what the church was giving me. I was so broke during Christmas I could not even afford a $10 Christmas tree. This brought a strain on

Man eating in Japan

142

my wife and our relationship, but my darling wife stuck it out. I knew she felt the pressure of not having enough income to buy some of the basic things we needed, but some how we made it; due largely to the magic of a virtuous woman.

Early one summer morning in July, a young man who had a notorious history of drug addiction called me to take him to look for employment. He was trying to make a new start in life after=receiving Christ as his Savior. So naturally I was compelled to help him, even though I needed help. I took him to the employment office and while I was there, I decided to look at the job openings. To my surprise, I saw a Photographer's job listed. This excited me, I asked the clerk about the job, and she said that the job had been listed for quite some time and that she was surprised that ~~not~~ it was still open. Photography! My forte'! It was a part-time job in Bremerton at Bangor Submarine Base. This was just what I needed, a part-time job. I was so excited; I went to the human resources office on base that same day.

Boy with snake in India

I met with the people. I was talking so fast that they had to tell me to slow down. I needed this job! They hired me immediately! It is almost like the job was waiting for me. I was a Navy photographer and now I was a civilian photographer on a Navy base. What a natural fit!

143

The Navy had contracted Pam AM to do the photo journal work on the base. This was just right

Door at Hotel in India

for me. I found out that if I were a permanent employee, I could take advantage of the travel benefits. I discovered that this was a privilege for employees having more than three months with the company. My employment was a day short of three months. I got the picture. I was determined to let my supervisor know what my desire was. I talked loud when he came around. I would say, "It sure would be nice if I could take my wife to Hong Kong." He would pass me as if he did not hear what I said. I knew he heard me, because we were only several feet apart. I threw other hints and was sure he was tired of hearing my vicarious dreams. My first three months were about to end when I noticed that some of my co-workers were given their pink slips. I knew that my time was drawing near. I feared that my hopes for Hong Kong would be another one of disappointment to my wife.

Lady in Market place

When my supervisor called me to the office, I knew this was it. The old, "Thank you for your service"

144

speech and good bye.

Instead, he asked, "Where did you say you wanted to take your wife?"

Linda entrance to hotel london

With a shocked look on my face, I said, "Hong Kong."

He looked at me with a smile on his face and said, "You have been doing a good job for us and I have decided to keep you on long enough to let you qualify for the flight benefit.

I said, "Now I can take my wife to Hong Kong to reward her for the suffering she has gone through with me."

He said, "You not only can fly to Hong Kong, you can take your wife anywhere PAN AM flies.

It did not take me long to know I was being favored. I said, "I want to take my wife around the world." I knew this was an ambitious request, but I am a dreamer.

He said, "Bring your itinerary to me and I will get the tickets." Then he said, "By the way, you have to have your travel completed within 30 days of your employment and you only have to pay the tax on the tickets." The tax was $200.

Here I am with the opportunity of a lifetime...and with a time limit. The questions now were: where we will go, which hotels, and how

145

much spending money would we need? This was almost like being given a million dollars of confederate money…worthless.

The Atlas and PAM AM flight schedules were my tools for mapping my journey around the world. For accessibility to the airports, I chose Great Britain, Germany, Turkey, Pakistan, Indian, Japan, and China as well as USA Hawaii. As we chose the countries, it was important for us to live in the comfort of five-star hotels. I made a list of the hotels in each of the cities we were to travel and selected the best ones.

One of the additional benefits offered was a 50% discount on the hotel rooms. The only thing we had to show was a letter identifying us as employees of PAN AM. I read the letter and the contents of the letter implied we were important people. The cost of the hotels totaled $1,500. The food was factored in for about $800 and of course spending money $1,000. I had to buy film in advance of the trip that cost $700. The total I needed for the trip was $3,700. It may as well have been a million dollars, because I did not have a dime or a job. The cost still was a great deal for the trip of our life. The small congregation where I was pastor was supportive but they could only give a small portion of the cost. However, others that

Linda getting Taxi in London

146

were excited for me gave another portion of the cost. I needed $1,400 dollars to complete the budgeted cost and time was running out! It was almost time to take our first flight to New York to and start our journey. With less than a week to go, I was in my garage and stumbled upon a lost damaged negative. I carefully picked it up to keep from damaging it further. I examined the negative: holding it up toward the light. It was a

Portrait of the late Bishop R. E. Altheimer; taken years before. This was one of the last portraits Bishop had taken several years before he died. The unique thing about it was that only the edge of the negative had been damaged from the water that flooded my home some months earlier. Immediately, an idea flooded my mind. From the negative I printed an 8x10 portrait. I knew his son, who

was a prominent businessman in the community would be interested in his father's portrait.

I walked into his office knowing I had something he wanted, but I had never sold a photo for $1,400. I was nervous. As he looked at the photo I talked about the trip and what I needed to make it happen, and why I was going at a time when I was financially unprepared. He seemed as if

Linda in front of castle in London

147

he wasn't listening, as he was engrossed in the photo of his father. So when I got to the money part, I asked him to loan me the money.

He asked, "Can you enlarge the portrait to the size of the picture on the wall?" He was pointing at a picture that was about 16" x 24."

I said, "I can make it any size you want."

Three days until day one of the 29,000 air miles journey. My faith was soaring as I counted the money. I knew it had to be God who touched the hearts of the people that contributed to the "poor man's" vacation plan. The tickets were "open" tickets that meant that we could stay as long as we wanted to in each country that we visited; and we did not have to make reservations to fly from each city, but we had to show up at the airport and if there was room on the plane we could fly. This was great, because we did not know if were going to like a place until we got there.

Knight Armor in London

For example, we arrived in Frankfort, Germany in the morning, after visiting downtown and having lunch we decided that was enough, so we left that evening. It reminded me of Washington, raining and gray. We stayed longer in places that motivated our interest. Often we flew first class between countries. I welcomed first class: the seats were larger and the service was excellent. We would sleep on those long eight or more hour flights and when we woke up, we were ready for another venture (adventure) in another country.

London was our first stop. We landed at Heathrow Airport. It was exciting: my wife and I together on foreign soil for the first time. We really did not know what to do even though we had mapped out our agenda. We were unfamiliar with the transportation system and the money exchange. We did what we saw most people doing, getting in those shining black cars that were shaped like boxes. You go to the curb and raise your hand, and there they were at your service. Looking like we were foreign dignitaries, we went to the curb, I raised my hand and quickly this black shiny car pulls to the curb and the door opens. As we were getting in I noticed the cab was already occupied. The passenger was an elegant looking white middle-aged woman. She looked like a movie star from the silver screen, or she looked like a silver

London Bridge

screen movie star, with her expensive looking fox around her neck. She smartly gestured to the driver and with an American English accent said. "To the Hilton please."

The driver turned to me with his distinguished British accent and said, "Sir, where too?"

I was too proud to ask him if there was a "Motel 6" chain where they leave the light on for you, so I replied with my mimicked British accent. "To the Hilton, please."

We arrived at the Hilton in downtown London. The Lady got out and gave the driver money for the service. I was trying to see what she gave him. I wasn't familiar with the money or the pounds in London. I saw what I thought she gave and I gave that to the driver, too. He had a smile on his face. I assume I gave him enough. This was definitely a first class hotel; it looked like where the rich and famous stayed. My wife and I walked up to the registration desk dragging our multiple bags suggesting we did not know how to pack. After all we were going around the world we did not know whether we would need long johns or shorts, so we had clothes for every climate.

I showed the registrar my VIP letter and he said, "Of course, I have a room for you." The letter really worked. He said the room would cost -----£ with the discount. I did not know how much that was in American currency, but I knew it was more than what I budgeted for. Then he asked, "How many nights will you be staying with us?"

He had told me it was____pounds which was equivalent to $200 in American money with the discount. I wanted to ask what it would cost for a half night. I did not have the nerve to just walk out so after settling down in the room, I got my contact list out and searched to see if I had anyone from London. This was a time when my networking paid off. I found a family I had met in Memphis earlier during Church of God In Christ Convocation. I phoned them ~~my~~ and told them our plight. They came to pick us up the next day. We were saved from an economic disaster the first day of our journey; the family treated us with great respect. It was good to hear the British accent of people who looked just like us. I noticed that most of the black population there were from Africa and the West Indies.

It was quite nice to see the British and the Black cultures interact. At "high noon" we were invited to have tea biscuits. They brought a cup of tea with milk and a small cookie-looking thing. I was expecting the tea, but what happened to the biscuit? This did not look like what my grandmother used to make, large brown circular baked dough oozing with melted butter. I wasn't sure what to do with the milk either. Well, I decided to drink up and bite. And it was a bite. Because the small cookie called a biscuit was easily consumed with one bite. They arranged a sightseeing tour of London via the public transportation. We enjoyed riding on the top of the large red bus looking at the sites of London while Sister Brown's daughter pointed out the sites as she explained the history of each with her beautiful accent. It was soon time to eat... where are we going to treat our most generous host? Will it be some of the up scale restaurants we saw during the tour, or will it be a place of their choosing? I asked if they knew of anyplace to eat and they could not recommend any place in the downtown area. I could tell that they were being modest without telling me that they were on a lean budget just like we were. I quickly remembered seeing a familiar site: the red and white sign saying

Boats in Hong Kong Harbor

"Wendy's." I had never eaten at Wendy's before. It was strange eating an American Hamburger in London's Square. It would have made a great Ad for Wendy's, "Don't be a square in London's Square, have a Wendy's Burger while you are there." That has a selling ring to it! "Don't you think, my love? This "my love" thing was equal to "what's up homey" in my neighborhood in Yankee land. When I first heard "may I help you, my love" I was sure I was being flirted with until I noticed the

152

lady said that to even the children that came into the store. After eating our foreign hamburger we continued walking around the market place.

Somehow, I strayed from my wife who was with the lady. I heard someone trying to get my attention; gesturing with his hand as if to say come over here. He looked like a mob character from an old 1950 movie. I was very skeptical as I slowly approached him.

He said, "I got something you 'ought to' see," as he spoke without moving his lips, He reached in his pocket and removed a brown leather pouch. He continued, "I got these and I got to get rid of them." My first impression was that he was going to try and sell me dope, but when he opened the pouch my eyes were blinded by the glitter from the diamonds he showed me. Then he said, "I give you a good deal."

I thought for moment, "This must be why God brought me over here on $200 to buy a million dollars worth of diamonds for a $100 dollar." What a blessing! I hit the jackpot. For a second, I saw myself checking back in the Hilton being escorted to the Penthouse suite on the top floor. Suddenly, a voice of reality called my name, it was my wife realizing the scam she pulled me away... from being a lollypop, or is it a "sucker." As we continued the tour on public transportation, I wondered if those were real diamonds. It was amazing how many people that we met thought we were wealthy American tourists. They did not know we were counting our pennies each day. As time came for us to leave London and continue our journey, we were saddened for we had made new friends we were leaving...perhaps never to see them again.

On to Frankfort, Germany! This was the shortest of all the flights. it was only ----hours. Wouldn't you know it, on the shortest flight they had first class window seats available. The weather reminded me of good old Washington, rain. I knew this would be a short stay. We took public transportation downtown just to say we had been to Frankfort. Walking through the busy streets, I saw some delicious looking pastry through the window of a German pastry shop. I tried to coax my wife to use her knowledge of the German language to ask the shop owner for a pastry I had spotted in the window. After all, she had lived in Germany during the time her father was in the Army in the 70's.

She felt a little uncomfortable, so I tried with, "I veta seen and speceting Deutch."

The shop owner knew I did not have a clue of what I was saying. So she asked me to point at what I wanted. Biting into what I expected to be a sweet tasting dessert, it was just like a biscuit. I found out that the pastry in America is much sweeter than German

pastry. The people seemed to be as bland as the pastry. Maybe because we came on the day that influenced the mood of the people, gray.

Boat houses in the Hong Kong Harbor

Hong Kong here we come! Hong Kong was the one place on our itinerary that I had been before for rest and relaxation during my tour in the Navy; now it was a promise I had kept to my wife. From the air it looked like Tokyo all lit up. We landed on this runway that happened to be an island. Water bordered both sides of the strip. While taxiing to the gate I got the attention of the flight attendant to ask to speak to the captain. I figured that we since we were working for the same company (at least thought we worked for same company) they would give me the name of the place they were going to stay; so I could go with them to the hotel and get the same discount. The Captain told me he did not know where they were going to stay. I could tell he did not want to be bothered, so we left them and looked around on our own.

155

Fishing for food Hong Kong

While exiting the airport, we noticed a sign giving the direction to a hotel that was on the premises. We were anticipating disappointing news, because we did not have reservation and the hotel looked to be a five star hotel; we knew our budget wasn't a five star budget, but it was in walking distance, so we gave it a try. We immediately drew the attention of the people at the counter. Others were standing and waiting but they called us to the counter. I almost looked around to see if they were talking to us, but the bright smile of the manager let me know we were among friends.

I gave him our PAN AM "letter" and he quickly read it, saying, "Mr. and Mrs. Penton, we have just the room for you please follow me." The bellboy quickly picked up our bags as we were ushered to an elevator going up and up to our room. The door was opened and Wow! What a room! A circular bed, satin sheets, and surround sound speakers. It looked like a penthouse: with all the amenities of the rich and famous. I wanted to ask if they were sure this was the right room. They must have picked up on something I had said: it was the month of our wedding anniversary and that was our

156

honeymoon suite. The bellboy said, "Anything you want, just call the desk." After he left, I looked in disbelief at the invoice to verify whether we were in the right room. It was the right room all right, but the best surprise was the price of the room. $33 per night! This was just right for our budget. We knew then that we would spend five days in Hong Kong. I looked at the wife with joy after testing the comfortable bed. We got comfortable and ordered our meal from the elegant menu. And in short order, there was a knock on the door: room service had arrived with all the splendor of royalty. The tablecloth was starched as stiff as the linen you would find in the "White House". The silverware was not silver, it was gold and the plates were trimmed in gold suggesting that they were the upper elegant china. We were living it up. They had all kinds of alcoholic beverages just for the taking.

I looked at my wife with a mischievous thought, as if to say "Why not?" My wife's nonverbal communication spoke very loudly. I was saved from another disaster and we drank coke instead. After sleeping like royalty, we were rested and ready to go sightseeing and shopping. I couldn't wait to impress my wife with my patent Chinese phrase, "Mo Chi Pay no whom so chi." It means, "I have no money, why don't you give it to me for free." You can imagine how well that was received by the Chinese. It got more laughs from the vendors. I wasn't sure if they were laughing at the fact that my Chinese was suspect or they had never

157

seen a broke American. Well, it was a great conversation piece.

We got a cab to take us to downtown Hong Kong. I asked the driver what it would cost for the trip, he said in broken English. "No speak English." We got in, thinking it could not cost that much. When we arrived, I pulled from my pocket several Hong Kong dollars and gave it to the driver who suddenly spoke fluent English, "That will be ten dollars more." My "Mo chi" routine did not work with him.

Hong Kong is a shopper's paradise, every kind of store from electronics to primitive woodcarvings were right at our fingertips. The only thing we needed was money. The stores that had the dollar gadgets attracted me and the clothes were my wife's interest. Bargaining for the best price was normal from store to store. We were very good at it when we worked as a team. My wife was the "bad cop" and I was the "good cop". When she'd see me about to agree with the price she would step in as if to stop me. This encouraged the vendor to reconsider and lower his price. It worked. We thought we were really getting the best of the vendor, but I wondered at the end of the day when we had so many shopping bags filled with electronic gadgets and clothes. I was so happy to be able to buy my wife some of the most beautiful dresses around. We had to get extra luggage to carry our new purchases. We met a black couple that we thought was from America, but soon discovered they were from Jamaica. They were very friendly so we joined with them and toured. It was good to be with someone else, because it felt safer. On the days we had left we toured the Island and took a trip on one the famous si pans on the harbor. It was so romantic for my wife and I as we slowly rowed between the houses in the harbor. We noticed that the people lived on the boats. They had some of modern conveniences like TV and somehow they had electrical connections in their small boats. After our last night of luxury in the honeymoon suite, it was time to leave. I knew my wife was pleased because she seemed more comfortable. Especially, after leaving the shoppers' paradise and with money in our pockets. We saw other travelers at the airport while we waited for our flights to the next country, with the evidence that they too were victims of the merchants' exchange. As I looked around at the people in the waiting area, my eyes caught a glimpse of someone I thought I knew. I walked over to him and saw that he had a toy in a box he was carrying. I said something about the toy to strike up a conversation with him. He was kind of standoffish, so I said, "You look like someone I know." He answered with some reluctance, "If you watched the movies, you know who I am." For the life of me I could not think of his name, but I knew I had seen him in a movie. He saw that I was embarrassed, so he told me his name, "I am John Sexton." It still did not register with me, but he warmed up and we talked a little and he told me that he had made a stop in Hong Kong coming from the Philippines where he was making a movie on location. Meeting the rich and famous was a great way to end our stay in Hong Kong.

For a moment it appeared that we were in the same class. We both were Americans with treasures from the east gained by trading, but I am sure he did not leave half his budget in Hong Kong like we did. However, we were on schedule, we had made it half way around the world on half the budget.

Our next two stops: Karachi, Pakistan and Istanbul, Turkey were really just "stopovers" in route to India. The distance between Istanbul, Turkey and Karachi, Pakistan is about 3,000 miles, a flight time of five hours. Even they seemed very short, because it was an adventure. We had to deplane at each of the stops, because they required each passenger be searched and questioned. Our stop in Karachi was only an hour. This was long enough to have the plane checked and refueled. But the Istanbul stop was more detailed. We landed in the darkness of the night at 3:00 AM and were escorted to some type of compound by soldiers with mean looking weapons. It was kind of frightening when they took us in different rooms to be searched. It was like being in a spy thriller. Strong faced, rugged looking men with turbans and dressed in eastern attire, asking questions about the contents of our luggage. My charming smile did not improve their customer relations. I knew they suspected drugs from their line of questioning. I was sure that we did not have drugs, but I was not sure if they were not going to plant drugs. Here we are in the

160

middle of the desert obviously looking like Americans, we must be up to something. I knew they were more suspicious when they saw how much money we had, or should I say how little money we had. This might be what saved us for farther questions. I am sure they knew if we were drug dealers we would have more than "aspirin" money. They let us return to the plane after intense questioning. I felt a little violated. In order to get back to the plane, we had to walk through the makeshift airport waiting area that looked like the praying ground for Muslims. We had to step over people trying not to disturb their prayers. When we returned to the plane we felt relieved. We made it! I found out later that this was the place where an American was taken into custody for trying to smuggle drugs out of the country. It was such a famous event that they made a movie about it. I wondered if we had been wrongly accused of smuggling would a movie have been made of our ordeal. I can see it now, titled, "Where Are You Hiding The Cash"?

We could see the sun coming up as we boarded the plane. Just when I thought I was safe, I heard my name called, "Mr. John W. Penton report to the counter."

I knew I was in trouble for not reporting the film I had in a lead bag. I was ready to explain, but before I could get a word out, the man said, "We have a first class seat for you and your wife." I had forgotten I had asked about it earlier. We needed the comfort of first class so that we could rest after

161

being up all night with our brief adventure in the Muslin world. We boarded and fell right asleep and slept until we were awakened by the sound of the captain announcing our arrival in New Delhi, India.

The epitome of love – Taj Mahal

Chapter Seventeen

THE TAJ MAHAL

A cultural shock awaited us. This was far different than the Istanbul excursion. We landed in what looked like a pasture filled with people and animals. We were escorted to the customs area where hundreds of people were standing in line, waiting to be processed and searched before entering into the country. The area where we were had a balcony area where we could look down over the custom area. There was a lot of pushing among the people as they tried for a better position in line. It was a noisy crowd due partly to casual conversations and stressful venting.

We were in another world that was very different than the other countries we had left behind. I knew I had to keep feeling for my money belt to make sure I still had it around my waist. India had every indication that it was a third world country and I knew that the little money I had would go a long way for anyone that made their living picking pockets. Our line was slowly moving, when I heard a commotion at the front of the line. It was a gentleman showing his disapproval of the custom office taking his pocketknife. He insisted that the knife was no

danger to anyone, but they successfully removed him and his knife from the line. They were not graceful about checking your bags, just like the rugged men in Karachi, "just the facts please." No small talk allowed. We arrived about noon and got through customs in the early evening. It was an ordeal. Just

The Taj Towell

behind the gates was an open area that looked like a field of tents and vendors set up to do business with anyone they could. It was very hard to tell where the public transportation was. We saw various modes of transportation, from donkey pulled carts, to bicycle powered chariots and rickshaws that carried two people. My wife and I wanted to experience none of these. We looked around among the crowd and spotted a small portable shack like structure with a sign that suggested he had a vehicle for hire. It certainly wasn't Hertz or Alamo car rental, but it was a better option than the others. The energetic entrepreneur, with his dingy off white loose fitting Indian attire, greeted us with a smile. It was not a smile that he learned in customer service school either. It was a smile of a Lion who was getting ready to devour his prey. He must be legitimate we thought, after all he is on airport

John and Linda at the Taj Mahal

property.   He talked with us as he put our luggage in the trunk. He asked.   "Hotel, need hotel?" Just before we could say we had a hotel where we had planned to stay he said, "I save you money, I have hotel, just for you." Why is everything "just for you" when you are about to be taken? We got in the car with the idea we could tell him where to take us. We had started to leave the area, when I noticed the police was behind us with his lights and then another police came, we were surrounded. I thought we had done something wrong, I knew this was it. The Policeman came to the window where we were sitting and said, "Get out of the car please." At least he said please, this was a little comforting, because I don't think we had heard please since we had left London. After getting out of the car, the police pulled the driver aside and begin giving him a tongue-lashing in a language I could not understand, but I knew it was pleasant. Afterwards they came to talk with us and apologized. They knew we did not know what was happening. After taking our passport, in an apologetic tone he said, "Mr. Penton, you were in danger, the car you were in was not registered by the government. The driver would have taken you out and robbed you, or even worse,

167

The Taj through the trees

killed you." Then he said, "We will call for transportation." We thanked God for protecting us from possible death. From a distance we saw a small white car coming toward us, it was our ride. The driver did not look much different than the one we were rescued from, but we felt safer since the police recommended him. His name was Carmar, a young man with charming personality. He had the same line as the other driver, "hotel, I got the hotel just for you." I said, "Here we go again!" He convinced me that he would take us to a good hotel that was not going to cost much money. His suggestion was appealing, because I knew my money situation. I mentioned the Ashokaa Hotel that was listed as one the best hotels in Delhi. It was where President Carter stayed once. While in route to his money saving hotel, we passed the outskirts of the downtown area. I was making mental notes of the various buildings as landmarks. I had a feeling that I would need them in case we got lost. This proved to be very useful, because I saw the Ashoka Hotel from a distance a red colored building that stood out in the mist of heavily

populated city center. I lost sight of the Ashoka Hotel when Carmar turned down a street

168

that looked more like an alley, as I looked back trying to see where we had come, I could not see very well, because the dirt dry roads left a trail of dust obstructing my view. A few miles later, there it was sitting in the middle of a gated area, our money saving hotel, that had the appearance of motel with a one star rating. I was looking to see if there was anyone near or staying at the motel that looked like an American, so that I could get an objective reference about the motel. When we got to the counter to check in, I knew my VIP letter would not work there, I just asked, "how much are the rooms per night"? He said without hesitation, "thirty American dollars." I remembered what I got in Hong Kong for $33, but I also understood that I was in a developing country. As I was paying the clerk, I was relieved when I say a blonde couple coming from one of the rooms. I wanted to say, " I am glad to see someone from home", but when they got closer, I heard them talking, and it sounded like Russian. At least they were tourist just like us. The clerk clapped his hand getting the attention of several young men that looked like kids from the neighborhood to help carry our bags to our room. They insisted they needed all five of them to help with our bags. When we got to our room all five of them came in the room waiting for me to give them a tip. I noticed that each one had his hand out. I reached in my pocket and grabbed what I thought was enough rupee (India's currency) to give each of them. When I gave each of them a rupee a piece they still had their hands out. I thought I was being

169

generous tipper, when one of them said with dissatisfaction, "small money." I had just given them what looked like an American dollar bill. I was thinking I just blessed them with five dollars, until one of them told me what I gave them in rupee was only equivalent to one penny. I was embarrassed and increased the tip until I saw a smile on their faces.

The room was clean enough, it had one bed and a chair, and radio. I slowly opened the bathroom door expecting to see a hole in the ground for a toilet, but was pleasantly surprised to see a toilet that flushed. I turned the radio on to see if we could pick up a station, maybe a little gospel or oldies but goodies. The only music we heard was that of the country we were in. I looked out of the window and saw the lonely security guard standing at attention at the front entrance with a machete in his belt. I guess we were safe.

The morning did not come quick enough. I could not sleep too well. I could see every movement in the hall outside my room. The door was about five inches from the ground and I could see foot movement throughout the night. I was

Photo inside the Taj Mahal

afraid that one of the snakes that I had seen in the market place would crawl in under the door or something. I stood watch while Linda (my wife) slept. We didn't even undress. We got the call from Carmar as promised. He was coming to take us to the Ashoka Hotel. He sounded different on the phone; like he had been drinking, because I could not understand him very well, but I did hear him say, "we will be there to pick you up." "We" what did he mean by we? I soon found out, two turban wearing bearded men came asking for us. I acknowledged who we were. One of the men said, "I have hired a car to take you on a tour, just for you." I was confused and replied, "there must be some mistake, Carmar was supposed to pick us up and take us to the Ashoka hotel". They insisted that they had instruction from Carmar to take us on tour. I asked them if I could talk to Carmar, who was standing in a distance. They called for him and he came, but he looked as if he was drugged or drunk. Carmar said, "yes, these men will take you on tour." I said, "no tour, just take us to Ashoka hotel." They saw that I was serious, so they looked at each other and said a few words in their native tongue, then said, "come, we take you." We reluctantly got into the back seat. As we drove away, they kept talking to each other in their language. I knew they were in disagreement about where they were taking us. I had a plan. I started talking loud to my wife so that they could hear me. While looking out of the car window I would point out landmarks that I remembered while coming to the motel. I would

171

say, "honey, you see that building over there, that is

Snake charmer in India

the embassy and that building is the Ashoka hotel." I knew this would give them notice that I knew where we were. I noticed that when we got close to the Ashoka hotel they stopped several blocks away from the hotel. They started to insist we pay them $20 for the rental of the car. We got out of the car and I said I would only pay for the trip to the hotel. Somehow, we drew the attention of doorman at the Ashoka hotel and he ran toward us. When the two men saw them they got into the car and left. Again we were rescued. This was getting to be more of a "Raider of the Lost Ark" kind of adventure. The scene was the same, men with turban, dusty roads, the exotic music of the snake charmer, and the crowded streets. This is the kind of stuff from which movies are made. We finally made it to the legendary Ashoka hotel, a safe haven. It was a five star hotel with all the amenities. My letter worked at this hotel. This time when the clerk said, "just for you" it was just for us. What a beautiful hotel, the décor was all of the best of the India culture: art on display in the reception area, neatly dressed bellmen, fresh flowers noticeably

Linda at the entrance of Hotel in India

placed on the large wood carved tables through out the hotel. This was it. Our room was equally furnished and bed was dressed with expensive linen. We rested very well in the comfort of luxury.

The restaurant on the premise clear and had the aroma of curry spices. When we ordered from the menu, we looked for food we could recognize. My eyes honed in on the pizza. It was the only thing on the menu that was familiar to me. The waiter took our order and looked puzzled when I said, "make it plain." I didn't recognize any of the topping so I ordered plain. He brought the order. It was what I ordered. Plain. It was dough flat with red sausage covering and nothing else. This was my first version of India's pizza. We ate it with the understanding that it was food we knew. Being a survivalist, I learned how to make mayonnaise sandwiches with no meat and sugar water for by beverage when I was a boy in Bogalusa. I learned that when you are hungry, eat and shut up. The next day we found out that the hotel had cars and chauffeurs for hire. The cost was very reasonable, $20 in American money, for all day. This was very convenient and safe. It was just our lot to have a

173

chauffeur that was a registered historian. He specialized in New Delhi history. Not only were we riding first class, we had a historian who would give us the history of the places we toured. I learned that the ruins that were located on the outskirts of town and the story about the snake charmers were very popular in India. He took us to a Hindu Temple and explained the different gods that were sacredly worshiped in the temple. We had to take off our shoes to accept the blessings of the priest before entering. My wife was a little apprehensive when we were anointed with oil and our foreheads marked. I

Linda with Indian Lady

figured I had no reason to be afraid. I remembered in the bible where the Apostle Paul went to Athens, and saw all the statues of the Greek gods and he let the people of Athens know that the statues did not have power, but it was the Living God in whom the people should believe. During our walk through the temple, I noticed that gold was the dominating

174

John and Linda with Driver in India

theme of its décor. He pointed to a statue that had a tiger with a lady riding on his back. The tour guide said, "This is the goddess of bravery." They had a god for every situation: A God of this and the god of that. I was contented with the only one God represented in three personalities: God the Father, God the Son, and God the Holy Ghost. When we had finished the Temple tour the sweet smell of the floral necklace was so strong it gave my wife a headache. I guess the fragrance of the flowers were supposed to drive out the evil spirits. We continued our tour and drove through the market place. The road was crowded with people, however this did not stop the driver from speeding. It appeared that the people were not bothered by the impending danger of a speeding motor vehicle. They just moved without any fear of being hit. I noticed to my left a little ways ahead a crowd was gathering to see a fight that was developing between several people. When we got closer, I recognized one of them. It was Carmar, our earlier driver. He looked to be in dispute with those turban wearing guys. He recognized us in the car. I told our driver to speed up so that they could not catch us. After we got within a safe distance away, I waved at them. This provoked them to try

Faces in the Market place in India

and chase the car. I knew that they could not catch us on foot. We retreated to the safety of our hotel. The next day we took a bus tour to Agra, India, about 135 miles south to see one of the world's wonders. The Taj Mahal. We gathered with about 20 other people from the hotel to catch the tour bus. This was a small 25-passenger bus. This was the only date that was firm, October 15, which was our wedding anniversary. This was the providence of God. Here we were going to see the "Taj Mahal on our wedding anniversary. We learned that the Taj Mahal was built as a monument to express the love the king had for his deceased wife. This was a great love story. The journey was plagued with constant vibrations from the holes in the road. Every rest stop was met with a welcoming party of desperate vendors trying to sale everything from pet shakes to sex. One young man tried to get my attention and ask me did I want to take a picture with him and his pet snake he had around his neck. I backed up, so that I would not be too close and then I photographed him and I quickly put money in his hand without saying a word. We continued to drive through the rugged terrain, and then a sudden turn almost caused the bus to turn over. We braced

176

Our assigned Driver in India

ourselves by holding on to the seats. Before we knew it, it was over. I looked to see what was wrong and saw a large cow taking its time calmly crossing the road. This cow had the assurance that he was protected by the superstition of those that practiced the belief that a cow is sacred. I really wanted to tell the driver that my life was more important than a live filet mignon. We drove for several more hours and there it was rising out of the heat glittered sunlight, looking like an oasis in the middle of the desert. This was a real oasis; it was a white marble looking shrine that was so perfectly shaped and oh so beautiful. I could no longer sing the song that has the lyric, "I never been to India to see the Taj Mahal", because there was right in front of us. It was breathtaking. The peacefulness it gave us as we walked beside the pool of clear water that dominated the entrance to this magnificent sight. The people journeyed from all over India… just to wash in the pool. Naturally, I took my camera out: trying to capture the marvelous sight. My wife and I embraced each other with romantic intention. Here we were, in the presence of the Taj Mahal that was built by a rich king for the woman he loved. Now, I shared his riches with the woman I love. Boarding

177

the bus, we looked back to see this great wonder disappear over the horizon, the marble dome of the

John and Linda in front of Hindu Temple

Taj Mahal reflected the most rich golden color. As the sun went down, the marble monument vanished from our sight. All the adventure we had in India was now a necessary price to pay for the treasure of a lifetime. What a memory!

It was now time for us to leave this most adventurous place. I reminded my wife about the suit I had made the night before. The tailor told me with certainty that he would have it done the day we were to leave. I rushed to pick up the suit, as it was close to time of the flight. When I picked it up, I did not have time to try it on. I knew I was getting a great deal, after all, the tailor said, "I make the suit just for you." I grabbed the suit from the rack and paid the tailor. The "just for you" suit would have been just for me, if I had a left arm one foot shorter than the right one. I discovered this disappointment in the next country we visited.

I learned that, "just for you' is really the first part of the statement, if you know what I mean. Anyway I got my memories.

Japan is the land where the symbol is "The Rising Sun." I had been to Japan during my navy years, but I had not been to Tokyo. From the air Tokyo looked liked a well-lit Christmas tree. It seemed that every inch of the city had it own marquee. I had the address of a family who was stationed in Kobe, Japan, that was about 100 miles north of Tokyo. In order to get there, we had to catch the famous bullet train. The people looked like they all shopped at the same store. The men dressed in conservative color tailored suits and the women in their Calvin Kline business attire. You've heard the old adage, "we all look alike." This was certainly applicable in Japan. My wife and I were definitely an oddity being black.

Tokyo was the most modern city I had ever seen. I noticed that almost everyone had some type of electronic device that looked far more advanced than anything in America. Their earphones were connected to miniature music machines that looked like something from a James Bond movie.

The buses were so clean and equipped with digital cameras mounted on the rear so that the driver did not have to turn his head to see behind him. Everything was visible from the monitor in front. We were in a land that was already ahead of us in technology. The public transportation seemed to be light years ahead of the transportation system in Seattle and Tacoma. Even as modern as the transportation system was I could not understand the Japanese directions on the signs that were posted everywhere. I remember looking among the crowded bus terminal for someone I thought could speak English. It took several embarrassing interruptions before I found a man who gave us detailed instructions on how to catch the famous speed bullet train from Tokyo to Kobe. He also gave me his business card. He was an executive from the Sony Corporation. When we got to the train depot, to our surprise, we did not see many people waiting to catch the train. In fact it was kind of eerie; no sound of any kind. Then the train appeared from a distance breaking the silence. We positioned ourselves near the ramp where we expected the train to stop. What a sight...a shiny slick bullet looking train coming down the tracks that were so straight they seemed to disappear into infinity. The closer the train got to the station, people suddenly appeared from every direction like a colony of ant converging on a piece of sugar. The door swiftly opened as the people moved into an already filled to capacity train. We boarded, with the wall-to- wall business suited passengers. It was so crowded that we unable to get a seat. We had to stand and hold to the straps hanging from the rail mounted from the ceiling. Again, an eerie silence hushed in the mist of the crowd. Everybody was trying to avoid eye contact with the person within the inches that separate him or her. We didn't have that problem, because we were head and shoulders taller than those on the train. Even my wife at 5ft 4inches tall, had a height advantage. The travel time to Kobe was about two hours. The train had to make stops as we moved through the beautiful countryside. When we stopped to pick up the waiting passengers I noticed there were more getting aboard then disembarking. We had to move closer together as we boarded the already crowded train. It was so tight I could hardly move to see if my wife who stood right behind me. Fortunately, we were near one of the doors. This gave us a good view of the people as they boarded. After several stops I it became easier to reposition to make room for others.

One particular passenger still stands out in my mind. The one-and-only wrinkled suited Japanese. I could tell he had been drinking. His eyes were nearly closed and his head was down. He stumbled aboard as if he had learned every step and location on the train. I moved back to let him in. He still hadn't looked up. He simply raised his hand to grab the strap. Just as the train started moving he was secured by the strap looking like a puppet attached to strings. I knew he did not know we were next to him. He was mumbling in a drunken stupor. When he finally started to come to himself, he looked down at my feet and slowly raised his head; finally looking into my face. His eyes opened wide, as though he had seen a ghost. He started speaking so fast that I could not understand a word he said, but my interpretation said, "I need to stop drinking, I have seen pink elephant, but it is getting worst. I just saw a black Japanese."

He rubbed his eyes as if to focus them to make sure he was seeing what he thought he saw. I hope he was shocked into sobriety.

We arrived in Kobe in the early evening and met with the people we had met a National

Convention in America who in turn took us to their modest home on the Military base. Their hospitality was very timely and well received. We were coming to the end of our adventure and were exhausted from all the excitement. By that time, we had traveled for 20 days and 20,000 miles. There we enjoyed our first home cooked meal. After dinner we went to the local church that consisted mostly of military families. I was asked to speak at this small but lively church. I gave a message of encouragement to the congregation. They gave me a love offering in return, which was customary in the COGIC churches. The pastor had an idea that I needed the money, because I had shared my plight with him during dinner. Our funds were now less than $100. It was time to make a decision. Although Hawaii, and the Philippines were on our itinerary, our finances and physical condition turned our attention toward home.

The next morning we took the bullet train back to Tokyo without incident. We went straight to the airport and boarded the plane for home. We were weary after the vacation of a lifetime.

My wife and I smiled at each other with a sense of relief knowing we were alive and well from our 29,000 mile journey that had been compressed into 22 days. I tried not to think of what faced me at home. That is, the life saving adventure of job-hunting in the jungle of the unemployed.

Chapter Eighteen

BACK TO WORK

It had been two years since I resigned from the Tacoma Police Department. I wasn't sure if they had an opening for me to return to work, but I knew that if I didn't get employment soon, we would be in a dilemma. Although we were struggling with financial matters, I was determined to seek God in prayer about whether I should go back to work in the secular world. You know the so-called 9 to 5 rat race. It did not take a supernatural visit from the angel Gabriel to speak to me in a spooky angelic voice and say, "Penton, goooooooooooo... back to work!" The voice of wisdom spoke very simply, in the form of a rhetorical question, "Look in your wallet, what do you see?" I did not need to look, but I looked anyway; in hopes of a miracle; like a winning lottery ticket that I may have purchased in my sleep and conveniently placed in my wallet. The empty wallet, was a clear message, "You need to go back to work."

I looked for weeks, with no results. I remember praying at the church in Bremerton at noon. My prayer was, "Lord if you want me to go back to the Police Department, you have to make it very plain to me." While I was on my knees one

183

day, there was a knock at the church door. I went to the door expecting a church member who might have seen my car. But when I opened the door, I was surprised. It was a Tacoma Police Officer in his patrol car with a message from the personnel office, "John will you consider coming back to work."

You can imagine the excitement. I wanted to jump into the car right then and drive the 30 miles back to Tacoma to work that same day, but I held my composure and said, "Let me think about it." This was no time to be proud. I called shortly after the officer left and made an appointment to return to work. I found out that the person who had replaced me was a retired army Colonel. He had died of a heart attack after two years with the Department.

As tragic as it was, the timing for me was providential: both my leaving and returning. Even though during my time away from the police department, I had financial needs, it was the break I needed from the stressful environment of police work. I had the adventure of a lifetime behind me, now I was ready to resume my career in solving crime.

My return to the Tacoma Police Department was different from my first stint. I was more confident. I was a veteran. I was confident enough to ask human resources to let me start at the highest pay scale. I knew this was not the norm. The city policy was that any new employee should start four levels down, and then with time a pay level increase. I also felt that since they asked me to return to work, it would be in their best interest to make me happy. They granted my request. I was energized for months. I was always ready to do whatever was needed in the task of reconstructing a crime scene. This was a good time for the department in the area of technology. A French company was trying to break into the market of advanced fingerprinting technology. Tacoma would be the first city in the nation to have an automatic fingerprinting system, trade name "AFIS." We became a "test lab" for the system, which eventually came to be the most sought after Automatic Fingerprinting System in the nation. Through attrition, an opening for supervisor became available. I was next in line for promotion. I gladly took the position. This was interesting, because when I resigned I was told by one of the supervisors that I would never make supervisor. This seems to be a common theme of people who try to discourage you. However, being an over comer, it seemed to have the reverse affect on me. Being a supervisor had its challenges. Now, I was the bad guy. Now, I had to tell people what to do and discipline them. This always created problem. Being black compounded my problem, for I had to overcome the internal struggle of being insecure about myself. It was not always the people I worked with that imposed their assertion about me being the only African-American in my position; it was me... who had doubt within myself. Thank God for reminding me it was He who had prepared me for this.

Earlier, during the first half of my career with the Department was a bit turbulent for various reasons, but I considered those times as character builders. During the O. J. Simpson trial, I was always asked, "Do you believe O.J. did it"? I know this, that many have been convicted on less evidence. However, for the sake of this book, I am staying with the lighter side of my experience with the department. After all the title is, "I Ain't Trying To Be Funny."

After years of working, retirement was now a goal. The novelty of being the first black to work in what was considered a non-conventional career had lost its challenge. It was time to close a chapter that had spawned melodrama, with its front-stage view of man's relentless ability to survive the tragedies of life, to the thrill of uncovering the suspects who perpetrated those tragedies.

I was once asked, "How do the murder, the rapes, and all the horrible things people do to each other, affect your faith in God?" I told them it actually increased my faith in God, because it gave me a first hand look at what man would do when he is driven by his own passions. Man's misbehavior and its consequences are well documented in scriptures. Also working on the ground level being involved with people at the most difficult time in their lives, gave me opportunity to be an agent of hope.

Yes, I was there to solve crime. But it would have been a worse crime for me, if I did not offer the healing power of God's love. This was done, not by preaching to the people, but by empathizing with them: showing that I cared for them. I noticed that the simple act of caring during the darkest of tragedies is the best testimony of what Christ is really about: being hope for the hopeless. It gave me great satisfaction when leaving a crime scene, to see the victim at the door, waving with a smile. I felt more like the "Lone Ranger" leaving the victim whose life had been shattered with a since of restored hope in humanity.

One such time, was a call to a house, where a drive by shooting was reported. When I got there, to my surprise the victim was sitting on the bed with tears in her eyes. My next question was, "Ma'am, are you the one that was shot?"

She said, "Yes." She pointed to her right arm, I did not see a bullet wound. She was emotional in a different way than most of the victims. She was saying, "Thank you Jesus!"

I understood what she was doing, but I do not think the Patrol Officer did. I discovered a hole in the window that looked like it was made by a 45-caliber bullet.

She reenacted the story, "I was sitting on the edge of my bed praying, and suddenly I was knocked from my bed to the floor." As she continued to talk with a tearful joyous tone, I traced the path of the bullet from the hole in the window. There it was, a 45-caliber spent bullet on the floor. She was shot, but the bullet did not penetrate. The force of the bullet knocked her from the bed. Wow! God still work miracles. This was not the outcome in most of the cases. I never could understand why some people suffered more than others. There were times when it was difficult to reach the victim with an act of kindness, due to the deep trauma they had experienced. But I knew that a gesture of kindness could not hurt.

The graveyard shift was just what it was a "grave yard." It was very hard to stay alert and focus when you are tired and sleepy. Once I was so tired at 3:00 AM, I was stopped at a red light and fell asleep in a clearly marked Police vehicle. When I woke up there were cars behind me. I do not know how long I was out, but I could imagine the cars behind me were afraid to pass a police vehicle. They may have thought that I was on surveillance with some kind of night vision device that could see through the eyelid. I struggled, juggling my time between church and police work. I prayed for relief. I knew I was not pleasing God by being a human sacrifice...killing myself with overwork. I knew if I could hang in there a little while longer, I could retire with 25 years of police service.

Chapter nineteen

STRANGER

You can't judge a book by its cover, at least that is what I heard from the old "wise one". I agree with this saying, but my addendum to it would is, "but the cover should make you want to read the book." I know you can't tell what a person is just by looking at them, but sometime how people look motivates you to want to know more about them. I was in the restaurant at the Sheraton Hotel in downtown Tacoma, when I saw such a man. He was sitting alone and I asked, "Would you mind, if I joined you?" He graciously said, "certainly I do not mind, I am a stranger in Tacoma, it would be nice to have company." We talked for a while and shared with each other our abbreviated bio. He was from Africa and now he knew I was from a foreign country. Bogalusa, Louisiana, or at least it sounded like a foreign country to him. We left each other after a casual goodbye. The next day I returned to the hotel to pick up my guest from California that was scheduled to speak at our church on that Sunday. I saw the gentleman standing near the door waiting for a taxi. I went to greet him, and he said, "I am waiting for a taxi, to take me around to see

Tacoma." I told him I was picking up my guest to take them to my home for dinner and invited him to join us. He was so excited and accepted the invitation. It worked out very well for my guest, because they had not seen Tacoma, so I gave them both a tour of Tacoma while in route to my home.

My California guest and I really bombarded

John and Babacar N'Diaye and his son

my newly found African friend with questions. We became even more curious when he told us that he was a Muslim. This really made for an interesting conversation. I immediately started my selling pitch about Christianity. He smiled and said, "if you are trying to convert me to Christianity, I am already converted, I am a Muslim." I knew then, he did not want to be bothered with our Christian assault. I quickly changed the subject as I pointed out some of the scenic views of the city. I had called home to prepare let my wife know to prepare for one more guest for dinner.

At the dinner we shared many stories. It was a time of laughter and good fellowship. The time slipped past and before long it was time to go to our evening church service. I was reluctant to ask our Muslim guest, if he wanted to attend church with us, but I asked. He surprised me and said, "yes." When we arrived, the congregation was singing toe tapping and hand clapping gospel music. He sat on the front row and soon I noticed he was hand clapping and toe tapping too. He looked as though he was enjoying himself. After service, he expressed that he really enjoyed himself and that was his first time in a church like ours. I knew what he meant, "a Pentecostal church." It may have been his first time in any Christian church.

He had a plane to catch later that night. While driving him to the airport, he told me more about who he was and why he was

in Tacoma. He said, "I am the former President of the African Development Bank." I was not too familiar with the African Development Bank, but I knew it was big. With a surprise expression on my face, I asked, "is that anything like the World Bank", he said, "yes." There, I was with a man who has been entertained by heads of states, such as the President of the United States and was known by every King and President of every country in Africa, riding in my car and eating at my home. When I first met him, I knew he would be an interesting book to read, because of the way he carried himself, but I did not think he would be a best selling novel. He shared with me the reason for his trip to Tacoma. When I heard him say he was here to talk with one of the largest pension management companies based in Tacoma, to present a $500,000,000 proposal, it didn't take me long to know he was not interested in my checkbook. When he said, "my newly formed company is looking for investors in Africa's infrastructure", I knew my dollar was not enough to get the project off the ground. He said with sadness that the company did not accept his proposal. He was looking for each investor to give a minimum of $50,000,000. This was really high finance. He said, "I came here looking for money, but I found something more valuable than money...a friend." What an honor coming from a man of honor.

I sensed that he was sincere. I thank God for allowing me to meet Mr._____at that time in his life he needed a friend. I remembered him saying, "If you ever go to Africa, let me know and I will give you names of people who will assist you". It was my dream to go to Africa, but it was not in my immediate future. We exchanged contact information. He lived in Washington D.C. during his stay in America and traveled frequently to various parts of the world. He spoke several dialects including French, as he was born and raised in Senegal West Africa. We kept in contact via telephone. One morning I had a very strong desire to call him, because I hadn't heard from him in a while. When I reached him, he sounded different. He was sobbing. I asked him what was wrong. He said, "I was watching TV last night, I saw this program and they were talking about Jesus Christ, I was touched by what was being said and at the end, they asked the people who were watching to pray the prayer of repentance with them. I prayed that prayer and now I know without a doubt, I am a Christian."

I was so excited. A Muslim had accepted Christ. Wow! He said, "I have a problem, my wife do not know this yet, she is coming in from Africa soon and I do not know what to do." I advised him saying. "Don't tell her, let her see it." That seemed to give him some consolation. We said goodbye, but I couldn't believe this was the same man who had said months earlier. "Don't try to convert me." I guess not, because he is converted.

Chapter Twenty

THE MOTHER LAND

Golfing has become a great past time for me. Of course, I talk much better about the game than I play. Golfing really is a game that you are forced to play with strangers. Often when you play alone the spotter put you with others. It's a great way to network. I saw the picture of a young African man from South Africa in the local paper that was in America seeking a golf scholarship. This got my attention, because I was planning a trip to South Africa as a reward to myself for retiring from the Police Department. It was also a trip that would correspond with a Mission trip for the Church of God in Christ that would be taking place during the same time. I wanted to play golf with this young man and to talk with him about his native country. I inquired about him and found that he was being sponsored someone I knew. We scheduled a tee time. While playing we talked about my planned trip to South Africa. He asked, "Where will you be staying?" I pulled out a brochure of the resort in Swazi Land where I was to stay. He paused with a look of shock on his face, "you are not going to believe this, that is the place where my mother works." He asked. " When will you be going to South Africa?" I told him in several months. He stopped again and said, "this is too much, I am leaving several weeks before you perhaps I could pick you up at the airport in Johannesburg." This was a great idea. Now, I wouldn't have to worry about getting lost on my first trip to the Motherland.

I had one real scare in flight to South Africa. Within about five hours in flight between Amsterdam and Johannesburg, I had fallen to sleep, suddenly a flash of lighting came through the window and the plane took a roller coaster dip. You talking about white knuckles, I thought this was it! I looked out of the window; it was black, no light, and then Bam! Another flash of lighting lit up the sky silhouetting the heavy dark cloud, giving them the appearance of a mushroom after an atomic explosion. I had never been in the air in the midst of a thunderstorm. I have seen lighting in Louisiana, but this was major. The shaking and the rolling went on for a while and my prayers were in concert with God's hand clapping thunder. I was hoping God was not giving me one of those, "just for you messages." He certainly, got my attention and all those that were aboard. I did wonder what the tennis superstars, the Williams sisters were doing while we were being knocked around like their 125 miles per hour serves. They were in first class in route to a professional tennis

South Africa Flag

196

competition in South Africa. I would like to think that my prayers saved their lives with all those, "O'Lord Jesus!" I whispered.

We landed safely in Johannesburg and there they were: the young man and his brother to greet me at the airport as he had promised. He had come from Swaziland by plane so that he could drive me from Johannesburg to Swaziland. It was a six-hour drive. As I explored the landscape of this most beautiful country, my concept of Africa changed. I was looking for the television version of Africa, but I saw everything you would see in America: rest stops and service stations along the paved highway. It was great to see substantial infrastructure in a land that had suffered greatly under the suppressed apartheid government several years before. Now its best years are before it.

We arrived *John with Mr. Mazia at his home* in Swaziland at dust dark. There were the infamous lines waiting to go through customs. I had a flashback of my Istanbul experience . The young man took me to the front and said a few words to the custom agent, and he looked at my passport, stamped it and that was it, it was just that quick. I knew then that this young man had clout. He took me to the resort where I was to stay. At night I could not see the outside, but the room was first class.

I woke up the next morning to a clear sunny day. I looked around to absorb the beauty of the colorful garden that surrounded the resort. This truly was a place for the rich and famous. This was a golfing resort, the Swazi Sun Resort. I was scheduled to speak later at an Episcopal church; the young man's family arranged the engagement. As we were driving, I noticed the variation of living conditions outside the resort compound. Just like in America, the poor, middle class, and the rich. However, in Swaziland the neighborhoods were not distanced apart. But the kind of house you had clearly made a statement of your status.

I was introduced to the priest, which happened to be white. He welcomed me with a pleasant smile as we went over the program for the morning service. I was not sure how I was going to preach in this very conservative church. I knew that I was not going to get an "Amen" response from that crowd. The young man introduced me. There I was in the midst of people where the majority of looked just like the people in Bogalusa. Behind me, on the stage, sat four old men dressed in their priestly gabs with ropes around their long white robes. At a quick glance they looked more like the people from Bogalusa who wore the same kind of outfits. I knew they were the Fathers over the parish. I knew I had to preach only the word; unlike in the Pentecostal church where you sang and danced, while the people graded you like an Olympic judge. A score of nine received a loud "Amen" from the majority of the congregation. Using the Pentecostal's scoring system, my score would have been a minus ten. I couldn't tell whether I was making sense or not, until I saw a smile from the priest. I learned that it is the word alone that was important, not how I sounded or how I presented it.

Now, it was time for communion. The priest took their positions as the parishioners lined across the altar, but I saw only one cup. All kind of thoughts went through my head: dysentery, HIV/AIDS, and other communicable diseases. I could not refuse to drink from the cup, could I? When the cup was given to me, it did not smell like the Welch's Grape juice I was accustomed to, but it smelled like the stuff my Dad used to bring home in his back pocket. It was strong. I got my first buzz. I could feel it in my hands and my feet and it was not the Holy Spirit: it was that 100 proof cocktail. I noticed the priest was very talkative after service and the people seemed happier; that liquid spirit must have been working.

Golfing on Sunday? I guess nobody will know. After all I am over 10,000 miles from Tacoma. We had an afternoon tee time and my host was a great golfer. I could tell he was bored with me after the front Nine. I wasn't a challenge to him. His cell phone rang. It was his father. While talking, his countenance changed. He found out that due to mechanical problems with his car, his father needed him to pick him up. He asked me if he could use my rental car. I was very tired from the jet lag, so I said, "sure, here are the keys." I thought for a moment, I am responsible for this car, it would best that I go with him. I also would have a chance to meet his father and see other parts of Swaziland. He said, "My father is far away in the bushes." I found out that the "bushes" was the same as what we call the "country" back home. We drove through undeveloped areas, where it was more like the places I had seen on TV. After diving a while we arrived at an area that had a cluster of large homes with land as far as the eyes could see.

I parked behind a new looking Mercedes in the driveway of a beautiful white stucco home. Out of the front door came a tall bearded man. He reached to shake my hands and said, "I am happy to meet the man who helped my son while he was in America." I wanted to say to him that I only had his son at my home once for dinner and played golf once, but apparently he was that I had done more. I insisted it was not me, but someone else who helped his son. I guess whatever I did really impressed his father.

Entering the house behind Mr. _____ he continued to talk, as a tour guide would. He gave me information about the house and the furniture as we walked. I noticed that the house was overly stocked with food and furniture; it resembled food and furniture storage. There were several men sitting in the dining area, Mr. _____would speak to them in their native dialect, as if giving orders for some type of job. I didn't ask questions, I was just trying to figure out why he needed a ride. The car in the drive way looked like it was in working condition. Mr._____ with his heavy distinct voice talked about his success as a businessman. He said, "I invested my money in the ground". At first I didn't understand what he meant by the term ground. Then he showed me all the properties he owned. He said, "Besides the King, I am the riches man in this area." If the houses and the land he pointed out was an indication of his riches, I could believe it. It was getting dark, and we had to get back to the "Swazi Sun Resort" for a late dinner they had been arranged for me with one of the representatives of the royal family. While driving back we passed through a town where Mr._____ owned a motel complex. He said that, "I do not go to church, but I will give you property to build a church." I asked," where would the property be?" He said without hesitation. "Anywhere you would like." The sun had gone down, I could not see the land very well, but I could see well enough that near the city would be a great place to build a church. When we got near the Resort, Mr._____ asked to be dropped off at the beautiful gated community. I could tell, he did not want me to go into the gated area. We dropped him off and he walked through the gate that was farthest away, but I could tell that he went to the house nearest to the entrance of the gate.

201

House and surrounding land of Mr. Mazia in Swaziland

Awaiting us at the resort, were two beautiful females dressed in their traditional attire. These women were members of the royal family sent by the royal mother. No. They were not topless, like some of the maiden used to dress. The King had a harem of women. In fact he had nine wives. I assume these were from his harem. The young man introduced them to me and sure enough they were there to entertain. I left them in the lobby while I went to my room to refresh myself. I had to make a call back to Johannesburg to speak with a man regarding my appointment that the African Development Banker had set up for the next day. The meeting was to get more insight into what his business was about. I had never met this man, but his voice was friendly. He said, "I was expecting your call, I look forward to meeting you tomorrow, and I will also be meeting with my sister who is coming in from Zambia tomorrow." He asked,

202

"Where are you calling from?" I told him Swaziland, He asked, " where in Swaziland?" I said, at the Swazi Sun Resort. He said with a tone of surprise, "my sister has a stop over in Swaziland, and she staying at the same resort complex. This was another providential occurrence. I asked him if he would mind if I asked her to join the royal family and me for dinner. He gave me her name and the room number. I called. When this stately voice answered, I said, "this is Mr. Penton and I am friend of your brother, whom I am to meet on tomorrow in Johannesburg. Would you like to join us for dinner?" She said, "that will be very nice, because I did not know anyone here." I went down to the restaurant and asked if we could add another guest for dinner? It was okay. As we signaled the table attendant to wait for my invited guest, in walks this tall dark smooth-skinned elegantly dressed lady. I knew she was looking for us so I got up and escorted her to our table. She introduced herself saying, "I am Miss._____ from Zambia. Now, there were three beautiful ladies and a young man. I would be lying if I told you that the devil was not talking big time in my head. Here I was in a country that believed you could have more than one wife, so it would have been easy to justify. I worked up an appetite just fighting the mental battle in my head. This must have been a test to see if the Holy Ghost was working, because I knew what the flesh didn't have the power to resist. I knew when I heard, "just for you" something was going to happen. Why did it have to be just for me? I knew if

I looked or suggested something more than dinner, it would have been provided. There was a lot of smiling at the dinner table as we talked. One of the young ladies from the royal family complained of a mile toothache. I guess God said, "Penton you need some help." Perhaps I did. She didn't smile much after she developed that toothache. After dinner, the young man suggested we go to my suite. I said jokingly, "If you are coming to my room, you must come as a group." I know there is safety in numbers. I knew by myself, it would have been, "Hail Mary Mother of God, pray for us sinners now" and I would have had to go back to the altar that wasn't serving real wine.

We had fun talking and sharing our adventures. This was one of mine: being in a suite in Africa with three beautiful women. One of the ladies said, "you are not like Whitney Houston, she wasn't as nice as you." I guess this a compliment? It was time for them to go, after a wonderful night of entertaining. After they left, the young man came back and said, "too bad you are straight, those women really like you" and he left shaking his head. I guess he had never seen a straight man resist what was clearly temptation. I should have told him, that I had never seen a man resist such temptation before either, because it certainly was not me, it was the Holy Ghost.

Relatives and friends of the Royal Family in Swaziland

I woke up early the next morning about five hours before I was scheduled to leave for Johannesburg. I didn't want to take a chance on missing my flight. I went to the lobby for the concierge to call a taxi for me. He called. I waited...and waited...and waited. It was two hours and still no taxi! I asked the concierge what was the delay? He said the drive must have fallen asleep. I was desperate as I looked around the resort for anyone who was going to the airport. I was willing to pay them. I had hoped to go back to the area where Mr._____ had shown me the land, while on my way to airport, so that I could take pictures of it with my movie camera. I needed to document this blessing. Time was running out! I saw a small red car pull up in front of the resort. It was the same car I had seen the day before as it dropped someone off at the resort. An older lady was driving. I didn't care who was driving. I needed a ride. I approached the car and pleaded my case. She gladly agreed to take me. I got in the car, relieved and shared with her my intentions of going by the property that was shown to me last evening. She said, "I know exactly where the property is, I got lost in that area last night." She was driving about the same speed as she was talking, which was fine with me. After all it had been three hours waiting on a taxi. When I told her that I was a preacher, her face lit up with a brighter smile. She said, "I am Pentecostal. Hallelujah"! I saw the gate housing area where Mr._____ was dropped off the night before. I was not sure of which of the houses were his, so I stood outside the gate and yelled. "Mr._____, Mr. _____." Slowly, the curtain moved on the upstairs window of the house to the left of the gate. It was Mr._____ rubbing his eyes coming out of deep sleep. He replied. " I will be right down. He came down with his shirt unbuttoned. Being awakened, he wasn't in the best of moods. I got the camera rolling and asked, "Could you show me the land you were talking about giving me to build a church?" He looked into the camera and repeated what he had said before. I instructed him to point where he was talking about. I felt like a CNN reporter interviewing the rich and famous. I had to move very quickly I still had a plane to catch. I left Mr._____ standing outside the gated area wondering what had happened.

There was no waiting at the Swaziland small airport. I made it just in time. Somehow Mrs. _____ from Zambia had gotten to the airport and we sat together on the hour and a half flight to Johannesburg. At the Johannesburg airport there was a welcoming committee from the Church of God In Christ Mission Department arriving from the United States at the same time. This was great timing. It gave me a chance to see some of the people I knew from America. I was excited to know that Bishop T. L. Westbrook was one of the delegates from America. I knew he would be surprised to see me in Africa. I met with the party briefly as they were being greeted with traditional music and smiling faces.

That night, a severe thunderstorm hit the Johannesburg area. While reflecting on what had happened in Swaziland, God giving me favor with Mr. _____ and how the Holy Ghost gave me victory over temptation, I watched the most spectacular light show from God's showcase. I was not afraid. I would, "Oooh and Awe" as the zigzag lighting flashed across the night sky and seconds later the thunder would applaud God display of power. My heart was sensitive to the presence of God. In my heart, I heard the voice say, "I trust you." This gave me great joy to know that God was pleased with me. I could remember times when my actions weren't pleasing to me, or God.

I visited the shopping mall that was not very far from the hotel where I was staying. The mall was just like any mall in the United States. It had over 100 shops, and a food court and was crowded with shoppers. When I walked into a men's clothing store, I was greeted with a warm, "welcome to the

Motherland" from a shopper who was sitting in the store. This statement made me realize I was really in African the "Motherland."

People watching allowed me to see first hand how the people were interacting with one another. I am very outgoing, and I wanted to know how to approach these wonderful people. A smile and warm greetings get the same results in every culture. The people were open and receptive to my smile. I saw a group of young men who looked to be in their teens; dressed in ties. They talked passionately to each other. As I past them, I could hear some of the things they were talking about. They were talking about education and achievement in the newly established democracy. They were excited to here my point of view on the subject. I told about the programs that were available for the youth in America. As I spoke, the glee in their eyes became more intense. The young men had newly formed a youth organization that provided help for the youth in their area. They wanted me to meet their leader who had just left them a few minutes before I arrived. The young men insisted that I wait while they contacted him by cell phone. He said he would be there within a few minutes…and he was.

He was a medical doctor with a passion to help young black men strive for excellence. I told him that while I was in Johannesburg, I hoped to see Winnie Mandela. He was surprised that I had that level of network influence. I told him that Mr. _____the Africa Development Banker had given me permission to use his name if I wanted to meet anyone in government. He said, "I certainly know Winnie, I am her personal physician. Winnie Mandela was in deep trouble with the law. I was not sure if I should see her at that time or not. Dr. _____ and I became friends. He invited me to go to the hospital with him to see a cousin of his, who had been shot ten times the night before. His cousin was a victim of car thieves. The security guards at the hospital were reluctant in letting me into the hospital with my camera. The Dr. _____ persuaded them to let me in. The hospital reminded me of the St. Tammy Charity Hospital in Bogalusa, dimly lighted hallways and crowded.

After we had finished visiting the hospital I decided that I wouldn't be seeing Winnie Mandela. The next day I was scheduled to fly to Cape Town, which is a five-hour flight from Johannesburg. The Church of God In Christ Mission delegates were in Cape Town for the Mission Convention. The Delegates had hoped to see Bishop Tutu, but they did not have an appointment. This was an opportunity for me to use the influence I had with Mr. _____. He had given me the contact phone number for Bishop Tutu in Cape Town. However, I was in Johannesburg over 800 miles away, but I had contact with the Church of God in Christ delegates through Bishop T. L. Westbrook and told them that I could arrange a meeting with Bishop Tutu. I am sure they didn't know me as well as my Bishop did. He had enough confidence in me to tell them if it could be done, I was the man who could do it. I called Bishop Tutu's office and asked

209

to speak with Mrs. Brown, his secretary. I told her, "Mr._____ said that if I needed help you would help me." She said, "of course, what do you need." I said, "The Church of God In Christ Mission delegates are in Cape Town for a convention and wanted to meet Bishop Tutu." The phone was silent for a moment while she checked Bishop Tutu's schedule. She said, "he is quite busy today meeting with the heads of state from Great Britain, but he has a window in his schedule to take a photo with the delegates."

He met with the group for a photo. I could not be present with the group to meet Bishop Tutu. However, it is great to know that I was able to help the others fulfill their dream.

South Africa, the southern part of the Motherland was certainly a great place to see and learn about first hand from the people most affected by the new government. The Church of God In Christ Mission Convention was held at a convention center in a small suburb about three miles outside of town. It was interesting to see the jubilant way the saints worshiped. Their dancing was lively. The people formed a line holding each other by the waist as they moved to the rhythmic beat of the music. I was used to dancing in a non-touching fashion. The train would continue around the church wall, and with each round the line got longer. It was a compelling way to get people involved in worship.

This was a great time for networking and fellowshipping too. One young man named Steve Flan drop really stood out. He was a distinguished

Bishop Moody and Bishop Macklin and delegates at airport in South African

business looking "colored" South African. He had his family with him whom he introduced to me. I felt very comfortable talking with him. At the end of the meeting that night, he offered to take me where I was staying. I was staying in exclusive part of Cape Town: Ban try Bay in a "time Share" two bedroom condominium, overlooking two oceans: the Indian and Pacific. What a beautiful view. I was treated with respect, even though I was one among the first persons of color to live there since apartheid: which had ended a few years before.

Steve was quite impressed with the place, because he knew all too well how this would not have been possible years before. He invited me to come to his office the next morning. He said he would pick you up at nine o'clock in the morning. His office was located in the heart of downtown

Cape Town in an office complex. He was the director of the bureau of public works. One of his responsibilities was to entertain foreign guest who intended to do business in South Africa. He also had multi- vocations. He was a minister. What a treat to meet a person with similar background. I noticed that his office had various awards and monuments representing the countries he had entertained. One book cover bearing the State of Washington seal caught my attention. I asked if he would mine if I looked at the book. He consented, "Yes go right ahead, this is the book of the delegates that came from the State of Washington on a trade delegation a year ago." I opened the book and to my surprise, there she was a picture of one of the members of the church where I pastor in Tacoma, Washington. I said, "This world is getting smaller everyday." He did not hear me clearly, so he asked me what I was saying; I repeated it and asked him more about the Washington delegates. It was a strange thing to have this type of connection so far away from home.

He invited me to his home and to his father's home. We felt like brothers sharing with each other: our dreams and opinions. It was just like being down the street at a friend's house. Driving through the different neighborhoods, I could see the divide that apartheid still impacted in Cape Town. However, I was treated with respect, because I was an American. We went to one of Cape Town's largest shopping malls to pick up souvenirs of this beautiful country. A painted plate with the outline of the continent of Africa and a portrait of President Mandela was the souvenir of choice. Steven brought several of his partners that were in a private investment group to the condominium. I guess they thought I was a man of means, because they immediately started to talk about the possibility of me joining their group. Their idea was intriguing, but it wasn't the right time for me.

I went to the hotel where the delegates were staying in Cape Town, to give Bishop Westbrook an update of where I was staying. While there I met the great gospel Saxophonist Bernard Johnson from Forth Worth, Texas. I wanted the Bishop to see the resort where I was living so I invited him to dinner. He and I sat on the balcony looking at the two oceans. Bishop asked, "Who would have ever thought you and I would be at the most southern tip of Africa?" I did not want to interrupt prophecy by asking if the Bishop wanted to stay with me at this two bedroom Condo. He had to join the others at the hotel.

I joined the group again in Johannesburg to go with them to Swaziland on a private tour bus. It was a delight to go back to Swaziland. The group was going to Swaziland to visit a wild animal reserve. The bus ride was very comfortable. I slept most of the way. We stayed at the resort where I had been earlier. We were looking for spectacular show of wildlife; after all we were in Africa. Instead we saw occasional wild boor hog that was to be our dinner that night. It was a disappointment. But the trip to Africa made up for any hiding lions or elephants. I left Africa with a deeper appreciation for the people and its cultural.

Chapter Twenty One

THE QUEST FOR PRESIDENT MANDELA

Get Mandela was the assignment of our newly formed company named, "Let's Trade." Let trade was not two months in existence before it had its first client: one of the largest pension management companies in the nation. What are the chances of a start up company with a net worth in liquid asset of "one dollar" partnering with a company with 1.5 trillion dollars in assets. It was not only a chance it was a real challenge that my associate and I were given.

It was at the Washington State Governor's mansion where "Let's Trade" was discovered. We were there by the invitation of the Governor, who had invited some of the State's business leaders. I knew we were in a different league when we drove up to the Mansion and parked my 10 year old S-10 truck next to newer model cars of the other business leaders. I reassured myself with the fact that no one at the Mansion knew us so we had the advantage.

It was definitely a roster of "Who's who in Washington State Business; among, them were CEO's from the larger companies; Microsoft, Boeing, Azteca Mexican Restaurant and other business leaders. Everyone had their logos and nametags proudly attached to their expensive suits. We looked equally

Plate signed by Quincy Jones and President Mandela

John with plate signed

216

John presenting Plate to the Russell Company

President Mandela with Wife in Seattle for Fund Raising Dinner

217

successful with our freshly printed business cards attached to our suits. Our cards were so new that the ink had not cured. The name "Let's Trade" drew a lot of attention as we mingled with our colleagues in the dining area of the Mansion. Everyone was serving themselves with a variety of drinks available. I wanted to blend so I found a coke and walked around introducing myself and talking about high finance from a low perspective.

I was rubbing shoulders with some of the most successful business leaders. One tall white-headed gentleman came over to speak with Sister Melannie and I. He mentioned that he was an attorney for the Frank Russell Pension Management Company. I said to him, "you must know a friend of mine, Babacar N'eye the former President of the African Development Bank. With a surprised look on his face he said, "yes." It was very obvious that he was astounded by my knowledge of Mr. Babacar. We talked about his company's annual stockholder's meeting. He mentioned that his company was trying to secure a speaker for the meeting. He stated that he wanted someone famous. Without hesitation Melannie suggested, "President Mandela." He looked surprised and said, "that would be great. I will call you next week."

He hurried toward the podium. It was then that I realized he was the master of ceremony for the meeting. He went through the normal introduction, and he gave a motivational speech with a few catchy phrases. "We need you" in the state of Washington.

218

The next week, just as promised we got a call from the attorney. He said, "I would like to schedule a meeting with your company, to discuss a business proposal concerning securing President Mandela to be our speaker." I hung up the phone in disbelief. I felt like the little dog that constantly chased the train that suddenly stopped. Now what? I wondered if this was the way they were trying to make up for refusing Mr. Babacar his request for investment in his project for Africa. Nevertheless, this was an unusual opportunity for a fortune 500 Company to do business with a fortune 5cent company. We hadn't even established have a checking account for the company.

I wanted to impress our clients in our first meeting, so I went through my collection of local personalities who had a persona of success. I chose an Attorney friend and several other business people whom I knew would enhance our ability to pull off this project. One of the main players was Mr. Steven Flanders from Cape Town, South Africa, who was visiting me while he was on vacation. His presence at the meeting gave us the edge we needed to show them our connections were also global.

The people they brought to the meeting were several of their top executives, one of whom I had met before. She knew me from another event in which we had both participated. It was good to have a familiar face to help put me at ease. We talked about the strategy of the project. The idea of getting one of the heads of the State personalities was a

219

major concern of the company. Mrs._____ of the Russell 20/20 wanted very much to give us the opportunity, because she knew this would help us. She expressed to me privately, that she knew this was very unorthodox for their company to hire a company with little or no experience, to do a major project like the one we proposed. She said, "John you know we have offices in major cities all over the world, and we have people in government that could help us do this, but I want you to have this opportunity." I presented my prized souvenir, the Plate with President Mandela's portrait, to the Russell Company This was a good faith gesture: assuring them that we would get him for their meeting.

We presented a two part proposal; one part was to make the necessary contacts with our government officials to see what was the proper way of getting a person of Mandela renown status to the United States, and the part two would be put in detail if and when he agreed to come. The first order of business was the signing of a contract with our first client. The contract stated that we were representing the Russell 20/20 Company with assets of over 1.5 trillion dollars. I did not know how many zeros were in a trillion, but I knew this would get the attention of the people we had to see to accomplish our task.

We took a flight to Washington D. C. to meet with Congressman _____. He wasn't available, because Congress was in recess. However, we met with his chief of staff. His chief of staff was very anxious to meet with us when he found out that we were representing the Russell 20 /20 Company. He was aware of the power the company held nationally. We met in the Congressman's office. He asked with amazement, "How in the world did you get a contract with the Russell Company, this is the most conservative company in America." I could only tell him that God had given me favor. He said, "He must have, because this is unheard of." After he got over the shock of the mix match partnership, he was also shocked about our mission to get president Mandela as speaker for the Company. He reminded me that this was a large project, but it could be done with the help of the "black caucus." He became more excited when we talked about the possibilities and opportunities this could bring if we could do it. He took me to the office of Congressman Jefferson of New Orleans and Congressman Pringle of New York to meet with their Chief of Staff. He asked me to repeat the reason why I was there. I did and they all were excited.

It became apparent to me that "Let's Trade" was about to live up to its motto, "connecting people to do business." The Chief of Staff for Congressman McDermott said he would let the congressmen know what we were doing and we would be getting a call soon. In the meantime, we had our contact in South Africa talking with the South African government to see if President Mandela would be available. Time was of essence. We needed a commitment as soon as possible. We got an official letter from the office of President Mandela, stating that he was sorry he would not be able to come, but if we would accept an alternate in the person of Tabo Imbecile, the Vice President? We had succeeded in getting a response from President Mandela, but we came short of getting the man they wanted. The Russell Company did not accept their offer of an alternate. The Russell Company complimented us on our daring quest to get Mandela.

A year later President Mandela did come to Seattle at the invitation of the three largest companies in the State of Washington: Microsoft, McGraw and the Russell Company. The event was a fundraiser for the African Children Fund. Mandela is compassionate about children. I knew I should be a part of that, so I contacted the Russell Company to see how I could be there to get an autograph on the souvenir plate I had given them. They thought it would be a wonderful idea. I came dressed in my tuxedo with my plate in hand: mingling with the rich contributors at the gala affair. I had strategically positioned my self to catch Mandela on the way to his seat. However, I found out that he had gone another way. Then I saw Quincy Jones coming near. I knew he was a good friend of Mandela. The music was playing loud, therefore making it hard to hear. I got the plate ready, as Quincy approached me and saw the plate, I said, almost shouting so he could hear me over the music, "can you get Mandela's autograph on this plate for me?" He took the plate and shouted,

222

"Who do I write the autograph to?" He thought I was asking him for his autograph. I did not have the nerve to correct him, I just said, "to John." He signed it and gave it back to me. Now, I had Quincy Jones autograph on Mandela's portrait. I was not going to let this moment past without getting this plate signed by Mandela. I walked toward the table where Mandela was sitting and before I could get close I was stopped by security with my plate in hand. I told them what I wanted. He took the plate and told me he would get it signed. The plate was signed. Now I had Quincy Jones and Mandela's autographs on a plate that I had to give back to the Russell Company.

Things in life may not go as planned, but we are certainly better for the challenges. Remember to laugh at yourself before others do, it is good therapy for the serious ones. See the photo on the next page a message by what we can consider an accident. Remember, I Ain't trying to be funny.

The cross in Memory of those who died in 1942 Bataan Death March in the Philipines.

This is my mystery photo taken in Bataan. The double exposure was by accident. My camera malfunctioned while taking two separate photos of this man and the cross. Look at the results. The photo has spiritual meaning.

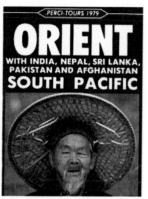

Photo taken 1969 1　　**Photo discovered 1979**

The above photographs are of the same Chinese man in Hong Kong. The photo on the left was taken by me in 1969 and the photo on the right I found on the cover of a travel magazine in 1979, ten years later.

Isn't life the same, when you think you are the only one with an idea someone else is also thinking of the same. Therefore, do not take life too serious, but be serious

THE INSERTED PAGE

It is 4:10 in the morning of January 11, 2005 and heart is very heavy. I feel that I should add these words to my book.

I realize that the stories in this book have a successful ending and that God hands can be seen in every event of my life. However, God is grieved by decisions we make in life that causes us to stray away from putting God first in our lives.

I here the spirit of God says, "I have spoken hear me now !". I do not know fully what this may mean to you as a reader of this book, but I know what it means to me. God is calling all those that say that they are followers of Christ to examine themselves and hear what the spirit is saying to the church. The enemy of Christ is laughing at us and I believe God is saying, " I AIN'T TRYING TO BE FUNNY"

Ezekiel 36:2 (KJV)
Thus saith the Lord God; Because the enemy hath said against you, Aha, even the ancient high places are ours in possession:

Please read the complete chapter of Ezekiel 36 you will understand what God is saying in context. Also ask God to speak to you as you read.

CROSSING THE PATHS OF MANY LIVES.........

John and Ahmad Rashad

John and Bill Cosby

John and Bishop Charles Blake

John and Rick Warren

Shaun Alexander and Shawn Springs

Charles Spikes and Cleveland Indian in the 1970's

Patrick Swayze on movie set for "Green Dragon"

Lesa Frazier-Page

Bishop G. E. Patterson

Billy Graham and Chaplain Morgan

Mother Willie Mae Rivers

Governor Gary Locke

Bishop T. L. Westbrook and Pastor Banks

Rev. Sunday Adelaja

232